# AWAKENING

From Hollow Religion to Heavenly Relationship

## RICHARD PENNYSTAN

RIVER
PUBLISHING

River Publishing & Media Ltd
Bradbourne Stables
East Malling
Kent ME19 6DZ
United Kingdom

info@river-publishing.co.uk

ISBN 978-1-908393-53-1
Cover design by www.spiffingcovers.com
Printed in Malta

# Contents

# Dedication

In memory of my Dad – who modelled for me a genuine relationship with God and a total intolerance for hollow religion.

# Acknowledgements

This started out as a booklet to help a few friends explore the biblical truth to understand why God was waking them up. As it grew so many people have encouraged, inspired and questioned me along the way, I'm so grateful.

To my Mum, Granny and sister for your consistent love and prayers for me over so many years. To all the Wicks family for being the best cousins anyone could dream of.

So many friends have cheered me on in this and added helpful insights and loving challenges: Colin & Natalie, George & Shellie, Jim & Dolly, Tom & Sara, Andy & Kathleen, Gareth & Lizzy, Adrian, Scott, Ryan, Stephen, Didi, Mark Hopkins, Tim & Katie, Dunc & Susanna and so many others.

Piers, for your remarkable generosity. Richard & Diana Scott, the late Mary Perowne, and Tom & Judy Parker for generously providing stunning locations to write.

Bishop Graham Dow for your wisdom, honesty and for modelling a continual hunger to know God better.

Stephen Backhouse, Johnny Douglas, Laura Sanderson, John Peachy and Simon Ponsonby for your feedback and insights.

Mark Stibbe for your brilliant help with the text and prophetic encouragement.

Kathy Silvester for your amazing eye for detail, red pen and patience with my punctuation!

Tim and Jonathan and all at River for your vision to respond to what the Spirit is doing rather than the clamour for fame in the marketplace.

Stuart & Ceri and all at ChristChurch Fulham and all the staff and church family at St.Chad's Romiley for waking up from religion with me and exploring these great truths together.

Finally to Nells, Luke, Jack, Caleb and Micah – you make my life joyful and complete.

# 1

# The Sleeping Church

A leader in our church called Ceri had a vivid dream. In the dream she woke up in a house filled with toxic green mist. She realised that we were all dying in our sleep, totally unaware of the mist which had rendered us unconscious. She rushed around the house waking up her family and members of our church leadership team. Many didn't want to be roused and tried to roll over and go back to sleep. But some who had woken up and become aware of the mist were urgently shaking those still sleeping, telling them to leave the house. As more and more of us came round we ran out of the building onto the lawn outside. There we coughed and spluttered in an effort to clear our lungs. We then rushed back to try and wake others up.

This dream happened to coincide with a time when we as a church were first starting to seek God to understand the principles of what I now call "hollow religion". The interpretation God gave Ceri was this: the green mist was the demonic scheme of religion, designed to send the church to sleep and slowly kill God's people. I believe this is significant; God wants to awaken His church out of toxic religion and into the fullness of what it means to live as citizens of the Kingdom of God, releasing the love, values and power of heaven on earth.

Embracing this shift personally has radically restored my relationship with Jesus. It has moved me from cynicism to hope, from criticism to encouragement, from selfish ambition to faith in God's power to bring new life. The shift itself dates back to a prophetic prayer appointment in November 2004 when the Lord revealed to a young couple I had never met that I had "picked up a religious spirit." When I heard this I recognised immediately some of the lies I had come to believe about myself and my ministry. When I repented of these lies and renounced their demonic hold on my life, my whole way of living, thinking, praying, worshipping and serving God changed.

Looking back on that day I see now that I had allowed myself to stray into a Christian life that was full of personal ambition, one that involved little genuine expectation of God's power and unconditional love. On the surface there was nothing wrong; I was happily married, a dad, and in ministry in a great church. But if I'm honest I had given up on the inside. I had allowed myself to believe that God wasn't really worth trusting. I didn't expect Him to change lives, heal bodies, reconcile relationships, inspire churches, transform communities and reveal Himself to those who had given up on Him. I expected Him to save a few in the long run but had no expectation of His life-giving power to be active now. I was therefore living a hollow Christian life. I was drained and frustrated because subconsciously I was trying to do God's job for Him. I was working hard, developing my gifts, debating theology and trying to manipulate our church into being better Christians – all so my ministry could look good.

In His mercy and grace God woke me up to the reality that I was saturated in religious thinking rather than living the Kingdom-building supernatural life which Jesus wanted me to enjoy. I had a form of godliness but my life was devoid of God's power. That prayer appointment was a wake-up call to turn back to God and be reconciled with Him and to make my relationship with Him the centre of my life and my ministry. Since then I have tried to cut off every fruitless branch in my life – every branch which isn't directly empowered by my living relationship with God. What started off as a warning against hollow religion accordingly became an invitation to be reconciled with God my Father, Jesus my Saviour and the Holy Spirit in me.

My ministry as a church leader has changed since that day. I have seen more miracles although not everyone I've prayed for has been healed. I've received more revelation from heaven although I hear in part and see in part. I've seen more lives transformed by God's love although I also continue to recognise the brokenness in and around me.

The significant change in my life has been an internal one. I now expect God to be at work in me and around me. I don't strive to build a Christian culture of "must" and "ought." I no longer fight to defend the theology and practice of my part of the church and I no longer settle for a Christian life that bears absolutely no resemblance to the supernatural ministry that Jesus opened up for us. Getting hollow religion out of my life has brought me wonderful freedom and given me a taste of what following Jesus can be like.

I believe God wants to do the same for all of his children and for us collectively as the Bride of Christ. The Father is preparing a Bride for his son Jesus. Imagine what kind of a wedding it would be if an ugly, critical bride turned up to marry the radical, generous Son of God! God the Father knows His Son and knows that He really doesn't want to marry a Pharisee. Remember what happened last time He met them!

I passionately believe that God wants to get hollow religion out of the Church. Since recognising hollow religion in my own life, I've talked to many friends who are waking up to the reality of hollow religion and its deadening influence. He wants us to help one another to understand and diagnose the hollow religion in the Church and to prescribe the antidote – living in the fullness of everything Jesus paid for on the cross.

Many of us have had an encounter with the Holy Spirit and a desire to throw off hollow religion but little biblical understanding of what it is. We have had little teaching to help our brain catch up with what our hearts have already embraced. That was where I was. Having repented of religion I then asked God to give me a biblical understanding of what I'd renounced. Over the next few years God thoroughly answered that prayer. I started collating notes from my Bible readings as I saw more and more how hollow religion is critiqued throughout the Bible. As I did that, this book was conceived.

## Minding the Gap

The comedian Eddie Izzard described his incredulity at the gap between Jesus and the 20th century Western Church when he said "Jesus was full of radical cool ideas but now we've got mumbling in cold buildings." Whilst it's true that renewal over the past fifty years has moved us beyond "mumbling in cold buildings", the green mist of hollow religion is still poisoning the Church.

I vividly remember an exercise at a leader's conference in which we were invited to brainstorm the various adjectives we associated with Church. We then repeated the exercise, this time brainstorming all the adjectives we associated with the ministry of Jesus. Comparing the two on a white board was life-changing!

| Church | Jesus |
|---|---|
| Boring | Healing |
| Stuck in tradition | Radical teaching |
| In-fighting | Miraculous power |
| Sanctuary for the lost and broken | Loving |
| Lifeless | Grace |
| Judgemental | Inclusive of all |
| Community | Resurrection life |
| Hierarchical | Forgiveness |
| A building for ceremonies | Defeating demons |
| Busy | Challenging |
| Frustrated | Relational |
| Defeated | Prophetic |
| | Revelation of God |

When these impressions of the Church were brought together, the overall picture was one of hollow religion – a stark and dramatic contrast to the life and ministry of Jesus.

As Ghandi pointed out, we don't always look much like our founder: "I like your Jesus," he said. "But I don't like your Christians." So my questions are:

*How did it get like this?*

*What happened to make the Church so unlike Christ?*

One answer is that in order to make God's family powerless, the dominion of darkness has been using hollow religion to weaken us. This has created religion without supernatural power, detaching people from the life of heaven.

Hollow religion flows from believing the lie that we are distant from God. Since the very beginning of history the enemy has tried to convince humans that there's a gap between us and

God. When we embrace this ungodly belief we live lives that are separate from God. We might still cling to His principles, values and laws but when we become detached from relationship with Him our efforts to please Him become hollow and religious.

All this indicates that the green mist of hollow religion is spread by demonic deception and its origins are in the dominion of darkness.

However, this mist can only send us to sleep when we choose to inhale it as a toxic substitute for the life-giving oxygen of the Holy Spirit (the breath of God). This is where human responsibility comes in. We cannot therefore blame it all on the dark side, as it were. It is a tragic fact that our sinful nature is more attracted to the green mist than to the breath of God. So often we make the wrong choice and opt for religion rather than relationship.

The reason we are tricked into hollow religion is because of our sinful desire to be in charge and to be like God, powerful and ruling. The irony is that we already have this position because we were made in God's image and given stewardship of the earth. A friend of mine has described religion as "trying to obtain what we already have." That's the tragedy. We already have the might and the right – the power and the authority – to reign on the earth. As children of God we are mandated to bring the rule of heaven to earth. What we had in the First Adam but lost, we have restored in the Last Adam, Jesus Christ. Since the serpent entered the garden, his tactic has always been to convince us that God is distant and that we need to work to become like God. He has sold us the "distance lie" – the lie that God is remote not relational.

## Minding Our Language

Before we start it might help to clarify some of the language I use in order to demolish any potential blockages to you receiving what God has for you in this book.

For example, there is a wide range of connotations when it comes to the word "religion." I've found that using the word religion in a universally negative way can be a blockage to many who see some positives in it. Some, after all, have had positive experiences of what we might generally call "religion." In order to be more specific I've chosen to adopt the term "hollow religion." This is a more accurate reflection of what we will be looking at throughout this book.

This book is not about attacking those who are different. We can all fall into the mistake of judging the worship, actions or attitudes of others, in the process creating a smokescreen for our own hollow religion. As one friend put it, "One person's breakthrough can become another's religion."

Hollow religion is not limited to any wing of the church. It can be present in loud and lively charismatic churches, liturgical and sacramental churches, and intellectually rigorous evangelical churches. Hollow religion takes a different form in each context but the same basic principles apply.

Much of the best writing and teaching on this subject uses the phrase "the religious spirit." I used to use that phrase myself and I am indebted in many ways to those who have taught on this subject; it has changed my life.

In my mind there is undoubtedly a significant demonic element here. The enemy right from the beginning has planned to restrict the Church by scheming to lure her into hollow religion rather than the supernatural Kingdom of God on earth. However I have chosen to use the term hollow religion rather than religious spirit for two reasons. Firstly, I have no theological grounds for identifying religion as a specific demonic spirit. The phrases religious spirit and the spirit of religion are nowhere used in

Scripture. Scripture reveals little about unclean, demonic spirits generally. All we know is that they are finite and toxic; little is revealed in the Bible about the hierarchy, structure or nature of the demonic realm.

Secondly, whilst recognising that there is demonic activity at work here, our primary tools for demolishing hollow religion within ourselves and our churches are based in personal repentance and the choice to replace lies with truth. Hollow religion is built when humans believe and act upon demonic lies. We need to focus on our part of the agreement and what tempts us to believe these lies.

The primary aim of this book is therefore to help you build a deeper relationship with God – one free from hollow religion. To fulfil that aim I have taken Ceri's dream as the basis for the journey that the Father wants us to make from spiritual sleep to being filled with the life-giving oxygen of the Holy Spirit.

So we will look at what hollow religion is and how it contrasts with Kingdom life. Then we will see how reconciliation with God – Father, Jesus and the Holy Spirit – can set us free. In the final part of the book, we will look at what an unreligious spirituality and ministry can look like.

Please therefore read this book as an invitation from God to draw nearer to Him based not on your efforts but on His love for you. I pray that you'll be able to recognise the ways that the deception about God's distance has crept into your life and that the truth of the Gospel will release you into new levels of the intimacy and freedom that God your Father wants you to experience.

# 2

# Religion Not Relationship

The ancient lie that we are distant from God continues to deceive us and rob us of our inheritance as God's children. The roots of this go back to the Garden of Eden and the events described in Genesis chapter 3. There we read that the serpent (i.e. Satan) approached Eve and said: "Did God actually say, 'You shall not eat of any tree in the garden'?" This immediately sowed into Eve's heart the lie that God was withholding something from them. Satan later builds on this suggestion: "God knows that when you eat of it your eyes will be opened, and you will be like God, knowing good and evil."

Just as the Word of God is like seed which finds fertile ground and grows there, the lies of the enemy are like seeds – destructive seeds. As in the case of God's Words, these seeds can only grow where there is agreement with them.

There is a whole raft of lies and wicked schemes in the words that Satan implants in Eve's heart, enticing her and then Adam (through Eve's report) into rebelling against God's love.

The lie I want to focus on is the idea that God has rejected them - that there is distance between them and God.

## The Distance Lie

Satan's strategy to steal, kill and destroy us (John 10:10) begins with an attempt to create a gap between us and God. In this he succeeds. By the end of Genesis chapter 3 Adam and Eve are banished from the Garden. But this separation actually began earlier than that when Adam and Eve began to believe the lie that God had rejected them. This is clearly evident when they become afraid of God and hide from Him. If physical separation from God happens at the end of Genesis 3, a sense of emotional and spiritual separation begins much earlier than that. Adam and Eve believe the lie that God has rejected them and that he is forever far from them.

But the truth is that God has never rejected humanity. As the Bible emphatically reminds us, God is love. Even at this terrible moment during the Fall of humanity, God the Father had in mind that He would send his only Son to rescue us, to bridge that gap between us and Him so that we could be reconciled to Him (1 John 4:9-10). Even when we first rebelled, the Father did not burn with a desire to reject us. He burned with love to reunite us to Himself, so that we would come running home into His tender arms (Luke 15:11ff).

Far from being a rejecting God, He is a reconciling God!

One of the tragic characteristics of hollow religion is the lie about God's remoteness. Whenever Satan breathes this lie into peoples' hearts and they agree with it, they embrace the ungodly lie of the Father's distance. This in turn leads to living proudly, defiantly, and independently from God. Every belief affects our behaviour. When we believe the lie that God is far away from us, then we start to behave arrogantly as if we are in charge, as if we reign, as if we are God. When we operate this way we collaborate with the enemy and create hollow religion.

## The Tower of Babel

In Genesis 11, the people of the earth decide to build a tower and a name for themselves. Their actions are a hallmark of selfish pride:

"At one time all the people of the world spoke the same language and used the same words. As the people migrated to the east, they found a plain in the land of Babylonia and settled there. They began saying to each other, 'Let's make bricks and harden them with fire.' (In this region bricks were used instead of stone, and tar was used for mortar.) Then they said, 'Come, let's build a great city for ourselves with a tower that reaches into the sky. This will make us famous and keep us from being scattered all over the world.'" (Genesis 11:1-4)

One of the significant features of this story is the human desire for reputation and significance, gained through effort and achievement. The peoples of the earth are looking for status and this is illustrated by them building upwards, reaching up to heaven. They have forgotten that God is the one who gives status and recognition and that He is our protector. Ironically, through their proud human efforts they reap God's judgement as He disperses them throughout the earth. This was the very thing they feared in the first place.

You see how this works? The peoples of the earth had started to believe a lie - the lie that God was far away from them and that they could therefore do without Him. They then decided to unite around a mighty tower that they built as tall as the heavens. Afraid of being dispersed throughout the earth, they gathered together around a great edifice that symbolised their ascent above and beyond the need for God. Their negative beliefs therefore led to negative behaviour. Their negative behaviour in turn led to negative outcomes.

## What Is Your Plumbline?

Why are we so prone to believing the lie about God's remoteness?

The simple answer is that we've learned to live this way. We're born into a world that has accepted this lie and educated in a culture that promotes it. Since Eden we have believed the lie that God is remote and distant. So even when we have followed a religion, we have always tended towards form rather than faith. We have conducted ourselves in both rules and rituals as if we are forever alienated from the love and the power of God.

Let's think for a moment about plumblines. This is a biblical metaphor based on an ancient building tool – a piece of string with a weight on the bottom. The plumbline shows what is true and vertical. Everything gets built around that centre line and realigned to fit with it.

This is a helpful and also disturbing image. Those who accept the ungodly belief about God's remoteness align everything in their lives to this lie. The only way we can experience realignment is by experiencing an awakening. We have to be awakened to the fact that we have believed a lie. We then have to repent of that and renounce the lie. Finally we have to re-centre our belief-systems by displacing this negative belief with the positive alternative - that God is not remote but relational.

Since recognising this in my own life, I have made a conscious decision to base every aspect of my life on the truth that God loves me and accepts me. In practice this hasn't meant hours of recording those parts of my life that are built on the lie that I'm distant from God. What it has meant is that each time I see evidence of that lie emerging in my thoughts, prayers or actions I have been able to label it as a lie and then realign to the truth that God is not distant and has not rejected me. As I do that, I turn back to Him in prayer, connecting with Him intimately and enjoying an intimate relationship based on His amazing grace.

## Christianity Without Relationship

God created us for relationship with Him. He created us in love, with love and for love. God is passionate in his pursuit of an intimate relationship with Him as His royally adopted sons and daughters. Since the beginning of time, His longing has been to be a loving Father to us and for us to be His adoring sons and daughters (2 Corinthians 6:18).

Hollow religion totally denies this truth. A simple definition of hollow religion is "Christianity without relating to God". Jesus said "I am the Way, the Truth and the Life, no one comes to the Father except through me" (John 14:6). He came to give us access to the Father. Whatever our ethnic background, whatever our religious or non-religious beliefs, Jesus came to open up the way to the Father's heart (Ephesians 2:18).

Jesus was and is the only Son of God by nature. He enjoyed and enjoys absolute and immediate intimacy with the Father. The Good News is that through His death on the cross He has paved the way back to the Father's house so that we too can come running home into the Father's accepting and loving arms. When we do, we become the adopted sons and daughters of the Father and we start to enjoy a relationship with the Father. This means that we can speak with the Father in prayer, enjoying a close conversation with Him just as Jesus did and still does. We can ask the Father, seek the Father, and knock on the Father's door in prayer. If we have the right motives, we can ask for anything from the Father of lights (James 4:3; 1:17).

Thanks to Jesus we can have access to heaven's resources and the supernatural blessings of God - restoration, revelation, healing, discernment, miracles, spiritual authority, to name but a few.

These we access through relational faith in Jesus and sensitivity to the Holy Spirit. As humans we have a longing for these things because we're designed to operate with them and they are our inheritance in Christ.

True Christianity is a love affair with God. It is about relationship not religion. Even the pursuit of God's supernatural power can become religious when it is done apart from a loving relationship with Him. Attempting to access heaven through formulae, rituals or principles is a characteristic of hollow religion.

Hollow religion is a counterfeit of true kingdom life, i.e. living as God's children. As such the characteristics of religion each have a direct antithesis in Kingdom (that is to say, relational) Christianity.

The five counterfeit characteristics and their Kingdom counterparts are as follows:

- Form not power
- Knowledge not revelation
- Judgement not grace
- Static not dynamic
- Wages not inheritance

## Form Not Power

Hollow religion feeds on the craving for reputation and building 'a name for ourselves' and it does so because, as humans, we analyse and judge by external appearance, by what we see in the natural. This is the opposite of faith. "Now faith is the assurance of things hoped for, the conviction of things not seen" (Hebrews 11:1).

Faith focuses on supernatural realities, on things unseen. Human thinking depends on external appearance and the assessment of things seen with our eyes. As God says to Samuel in 1 Samuel 16:6: "For the LORD sees not as man sees: man looks on the outward appearance but the LORD looks on the heart."

Throughout Scripture we see the contrast between the human focus on appearance, reputations and circumstances and the faith focus which trusts God's word above human assessments. Hollow religion arises when the Church builds upon human assessments and external appearances, rather than on faith and revelation from God. My favourite definition of this comes in 2 Timothy 3:5. Here Paul talks about "having a form of godliness, but denying its power."

This simple and profound contrast is one of the clearest definitions of hollow religion. Hollow religion is empty on the inside; it focuses on externals, on what things look like, on reputation and style. It is proud rather than humble because it acts independently from God and His resources and trusts instead on human might and strength alone. As such, hollow religion becomes a matter of mere form and in the process neglects and forgets the power of heaven.

Form without power originates in humanity's desire to be in charge (Genesis 3). We quickly learn in life that we can't create supernatural power in and of ourselves. We can only access supernatural power in two ways: through relational faith in God or through witchcraft and agreement with demonic spirits. The first leads to life and freedom; the second to slavery and death. Hollow religion is man's solution to doing neither of those, instead seeking to work hard on the form and make that the focus of attention, denying in the process the life-changing power of the Living God.

## Knowledge Not Revelation

In Genesis 2, having planted beautiful trees with good fruit including the Tree of Life and the Tree of Knowledge, God gives Adam clear instructions:

"You may surely eat of every tree of the garden, but of the tree of the knowledge of good and evil you shall not eat, for in the day that you eat of it you shall surely die." (Genesis 2:16-17)

God's design was that we live in relationship with Him – remaining connected to Him, intimate with Him, trusting in Him to provide for all our needs and that He would be our source of Life. We would trust Him for guidance, for protection, for wisdom and insight; we would humbly recognise that He is the greater being and, in submissive relationship, enjoy the blessing of all His power and goodness, which as His children we can receive at any time. We were designed for this relationship, it is our true home and in connection with Him, we thrive and enjoy life.

The tragedy is that in Adam and Eve we chose autonomy and self-rule instead.

It is part of our fallen human nature to become materialistic, hoarding up natural resources such as money, possessions, land, food, or whatever our felt need is for survival, status or comfort. We believe that ownership gives us autonomy.

God placed two trees in the garden and gave Adam a choice: to eat from the Tree of Life and enjoy dependent, trusting relationship with God, letting Him be the source of Life; or to choose to eat from the Tree of Knowledge. By taking fruit from the Tree of Knowledge we chose autonomy which meant relying on our own strength not on God's life-giving power. Pursuing human knowledge over revelation is the first step towards not needing God. It creates a religion based on head knowledge rather than a relationship based upon the affections of the heart. It creates a religion based on knowing good from evil rather than a relationship based simply on knowing God. In the process it replaces a passion for intimacy with a preoccupation with morality.

Dietrich Bonhoeffer's classic book entitled Ethics unpacks this:

"The knowledge of good and evil seems to be the aim of all ethical reflection. The first task of Christian ethics is to invalidate this knowledge ... Already in the possibility of the knowledge of good and evil Christian ethics discerns a falling away from the origin. Man at his original knows only one thing: God. It is only in the unity of his knowledge of God that he knows of other men, of other things, and of himself. He knows all things only in God, and God in all things. The knowledge of good and evil shows that he is no longer at one with his origin ... The knowledge of good and evil is therefore separation from God."[i]

In the Garden of Eden, Adam and Eve were supposed to pursue a burning intimacy with God not a lifeless and loveless moral knowledge. But the enemy seduced them into believing the lie that religion (based on knowledge) is better than relationship (based on revelation). Believing that lie resulted in them experiencing disaster. The enemy seduced them into taking the autonomous path, to grab hold of knowledge for themselves, removing their need of God and thus separating from Him.

In the world since that terrible choice, we have consistently elevated intellectual and ethical knowledge above the revelation that flows from our faith-based intimacy with God.

When our hearts believe the distance lie, we have very limited faith that God is close to us and that He will speak to us. Often when I've taught the new covenant truth that God wants to speak to all his children I've found many people feel condemned because their experience has led them to believe they can't hear God. I've prayed with many who don't believe they can hear God. Often they've jumped to the conclusion that God only speaks to certain individuals, whom we label 'prophetic', and that doesn't include them. When we've started digging underneath this belief, the Holy Spirit has uncovered some form of the distance lie and a sense of powerlessness to reach God.

This was my own experience for a long time. Through my life I have heard God's voice at different times and seasons. Other peoples' stories of prophecy, pictures and visions always sounded more exciting, clearer, and more dramatic than mine. I'd hear the testimonies of other peoples' words or pictures from God having an amazing response from other people and compare my experience and feel inadequate.

Now don't get me wrong: I go through 'dry seasons' and there are times when God seems distant. In these times I used to jump to the conclusion, I'm not a prophetic person, so I won't expect to receive revelation. This lie had taken root within me because it was based on analysing my experience and comparing myself with others, not living in my true identity.

When others lovingly challenged me about this - telling me the truth that all God's people are made to hear His voice and that He has promised to pour out His Spirit on all flesh – I had to make the choice whether to believe God's Word or my negative experience.

In the end I have had to choose to believe that God does want to speak to me and that I am designed to hear Him. As a result my sensitivity to His voice has increased, as well as my confidence that what I am hearing is Him – all this while I've deepened my relationship with Him.

The outcome of believing that we can't hear God's voice for ourselves is that we live by information not revelation and this breeds hollow religion rather than the kingdom adventure of living under the leading of the Holy Spirit.

A crucial part of throwing off hollow religion is learning to hear the voice of God. We remain rooted and connected with Him through living by His revelation, not merely storing up knowledge about Him.

## Judgement Not Grace

Whenever I have asked groups to feedback answers to the question 'What repels people about Church?' one of the first answers given is 'judgemental'. Many people in our culture feel pain because of their experience of having felt judged by Christians. This pain forms a barrier keeping people far from God.

Jesus was explicitly clear that our role is not to judge, nor to condemn others. He said, "Judge not, that you be not judged" (Matthew 7:7). He goes on to say that the focus of His ministry was not judgement but salvation: "For God did not send his son into the world to condemn the world, but in order that the world might be saved through him" (John 3:17).

A major characteristic of hollow religion is judgement and condemnation. One of the primary signs of hollow religion is people judging one another, resulting in rejection through exclusion and criticism. The knock-on effects of this rejection are division, factions, defensiveness, and the fear of punishment.

Judgement creates a culture of pulling down not building up. That is the culture of the Pharisees not of Jesus. Jesus presents us with amazing grace. Grace in all its profound beauty is more than the truth that we don't get judged under the law. It is the truth that if we put our trust in Jesus then we are not only free from divine condemnation, we are forgiven and accepted by a loving Heavenly Father whose arms are always open wide to everyone, however dark their secrets and damaged their past.

As we learn to live in relationship with our loving Father, we find new freedom and release in his outrageous grace. When we choose to live at a distance from him, we become burdened and restricted by the heavy weight of condemnation.

## Static Not Dynamic

In Mere Christianity, C.S. Lewis makes a simple contrast between what is "dynamic" and what is "static". He describes how God, existing in perfect relationship as Father, Son and Holy Spirit, is dynamic and not static. His design for us is that we too should be dynamic. This means being...

• Creative like the Father, looking to make new things, pioneer, try things out, to produce and nurture more life.

• Redemptive like Jesus, always looking to seek and save the lost.

• In motion like the Spirit. Every time we see the Holy Spirit in the Bible he is moving, or described using dynamic metaphors such as wind or fire.

The opposite is static religion. Fear causes static defensiveness and escape into the comfort of familiarity. When we believe the lie that God is distant and has rejected us, this causes us to retreat into a defensive, static posture. When we live in relationship with God, born of the dynamic Spirit of God, we are free to move and to change. Confidence and trust release adventure and dynamic action.

When the Church feels marginalised, diminished or afraid of an increasingly secular culture, she often chooses the hollow religious option, escaping into traditions and putting her energy into defending them. The result is that, in the context of a dynamic, fast-changing culture, the Church can put a great deal of her energy into remaining static and defending herself against the kind of innovative change that would transform society.

Moving from being static to being dynamic can be one of the

toughest shifts to embrace. When we have found safety in tradition, the shift into the dynamic life of the Spirit is a challenging one. It's a shift that requires us not to trust in the familiar but to seek a deeper relationship of trust with our Father, so that He becomes our protection and security. In relationship with Him, we are free to live dynamic and adventurous lives, restoring hope and advancing his kingdom.

## Wages Not Inheritance

The fifth contrast between hollow religion and the kingdom is the contrast of living to earn wages, rather than enjoying our inheritance. Tim Keller writes:

"Religion, or moralism, is avoiding God as Lord and Saviour by developing a moral righteousness and then presenting it to God in an effort to show that he 'owes' you."[ii]

A child of rich parents can enjoy their parent's generosity and provision and often take it for granted. Orphans, on the other hand, have no guarantee that their parents will provide for them and no expectation of inheritance. They therefore grab and grasp whatever they can take hold of, in order to provide for themselves, either to survive or to have power over others.

What we are talking about here is the difference between being a slave or a servant and being a son or a daughter. The slave/servant pursues a life of religion/moralism. The son/daughter pursues a life of relationship.

The trouble with the slavery mindset is that it is one based on earning wages rather than receiving an inheritance. A servant works to be paid; a son enjoys his inheritance and works to grow the family business. This is why Jesus rejoiced when his disciples at last understood what He had come to do – to bring about a transition in their lives from slavery to sonship. He said, "No longer do I call you servants, for the servant does not know what his master is doing; but I have called you friends, for all that I have heard from my Father I have made known to you" (John 15:15).

The key principle idea is inheritance. I continue to find the New Covenant passages about inheritance mind-blowing. The bar they raise for what's available to us as God's children is far, far beyond my experience. That is why the Apostle Paul became so fervent in his gratitude to God: "Blessed be the God and Father of our Lord Jesus Christ, who has blessed us in Christ with every spiritual blessing in the heavenly places, even as he chose us in him before the foundation of the world" (Ephesians 1:3-4).

Hollow religion, believing that God is remote and that his presence somehow has to be merited, seeks to earn God's favour and store up perceived credits with God. When we are locked into this thinking, we become preoccupied and bitter about the cost we are paying to serve God. The truth is that we already have God's full, complete and abundant favour because of Jesus' finished work on the cross. There is nothing we can do or say that will make God love us any more than He has already demonstrated – through laying down his life and dying in our place. As we receive this beautiful truth, we become more grateful for the cost he paid on our behalf.

Religion is an attempt to get what we've already been given.

Relationship involves receiving everything that Jesus paid for at Calvary.

Religion seeks to earn wages.

Relationship seeks to revel in one's inheritance.

I've swapped from living by wages, to learning to enjoy my inheritance. I thoroughly recommend it!

## Saying Goodbye to Hollow Religion

Like the toxic gas in Ceri's dream, many of us have become so used to hollow religion that we're blinded by it. As we begin to see the stark reality of the contrast between the hollow religion we're used to and the Kingdom life we're called to, we hear God's voice encouraging us to uproot and discard religion and choose relationship instead.

At the end of the book in the appendix there are some simple checklists, based on the five contrasts we have looked at in this chapter. They are designed to help you identify where hollow religion has taken root in your life. My prayer is that you will exchange hollow religion for authentic relationship with God and that you will start to enjoy the power of the Holy Spirit, God's lavish grace, His desire to speak with you, the creative dynamism of the Kingdom and the indescribable riches of our inheritance in Christ.

All these things are like oxygen to our spirits. As we learn to live in these realities, we inhale the life of heaven and exhale and expel the toxic atmosphere of religion. As we do, we find that like oxygen, these gifts from God, bring us life.

### Notes

i. Dietrich Bonhoeffer Ethics p3 – see also Greg Boyd, *Repenting of Religion.*

ii. Timothy Keller, *Center Church,* p63.

# 3

# Bad Trees, Bad Fruit

Jesus once said that you can tell a tree by its fruit.

Hollow religion seeks to separate us from God so that our roots grow not into the Father's love but into our own efforts, views and resources. When we try to reach or serve God from a place of disconnection from Him, we become like trees that produce only rotten fruit.

I am very aware that in recognising and diagnosing the fruit of hollow religion there is a real danger of seeming to judge by what is seen. I have frequently been challenged by the fact that in attempting to highlight ways in which the Church acts in a hollow religious way, I have myself leaned into hollow religion by judging others by external appearance.

But my desire is not to judge or to diagnose hollow religion just for the sake of complaining about things I don't like! My desire is to awaken you to the fact that breathing in the fresh air of the Kingdom of Heaven is a far more life-enhancing reality than wheezing in the green mist of hollow religion. My passion is to show you a better way.

One other note before we begin some diagnosis. It's much

easier to recognise hollow religion in those whose style of church (or churchmanship) is different from our own. If we begin to do this, we need to heed Jesus' parable of Matthew 7:3-5 about removing the log in our own eye before trying to point out specks in our neighbours' eyes.

The choice for all of us is whether we are going to become good trees or bad trees. Good trees are rooted in the soil of the love of God. They produce healthy and desirable fruit. Bad trees are rooted in the desire to bridge the great gap we perceive between us and God and therefore produce toxic fruit. The good tree is the tree of relationship, based on grace. The bad tree is the hollow tree of religion, based on law.

## The Fruit of Worship

When hollow religion infiltrates worship, the results are at best dull but can become divisive and ugly. Few things incite as much passion as styles of worship because it is so fundamental to the Kingdom and so essential to all who seek to serve God, whether from a religious motivation or a relational one.

When hollow religion infects worship, the focus becomes about the form and not power. The Pharisees were famous for the energy and emphasis they placed on worship and doing it just right. In Matthew 15:8 we find one of Jesus' most stinging confrontations with the Pharisees: "This people honours me with their lips, but their heart is far from me."

This is a profoundly challenging and very simple description of hollow worship: outward expressions which are not a true indication of our passions. Note the language Jesus uses is of our hearts being at a distance from Him.

Hollow worship becomes about form, style and personal preference, rather than an expression of love, honour and submission to God from our hearts. Hollow worship stays on earth rather than rising to heaven; it becomes about me, my experience or enjoyment, my preferences and my critique of others' preferences.

Whenever this happens we become consumers of worship, using it as an experience to alter our moods. This leads to arguments, criticism and judgement of others – all hallmarks of hollow religion.

In the Bible, worship is about God. It's to Him and for Him. Worship is His invitation to love Him more dearly. Our worship is our "yes" to that invitation. When we, out of love, express our deep affection for God, He in turn draws nearer and nearer to us, bringing heaven (the place of His presence) to earth. Whenever this happens we become selfless participants whom He loves enough to embrace us.

I love worshipping in a context that has thrown off hollow religion. There's such a joy on peoples' faces when they encounter God; it's truly beautiful. When people encounter God they discover the rich intensity of His presence which takes all of us beyond our earthly mundane lives into His purposes. They also enjoy the freedom that brings genuine rest.

Whether it's contemporary or traditional, liturgical or spontaneous, loud or still, worship that seeks to give undivided attention to God and longs to meet with Him is the greatest activity a human can undertake.

Such living, loving worship is the good fruit that comes from well planted trees.

## The Fruit of Evangelism

Many of those who don't know Christ thoroughly reject religion. The world doesn't like hollow religion and increasingly reacts angrily against it. People reject Jesus because they associate Him with an institution He actually came to reform.

A friend of mine told me a story about how before he was saved his now wife took him to a church meeting in a pub. As you'd expect every effort was made to make this church appealing and accessible. One evening a group of missionaries were being prayed for as part of the meeting. The Holy Spirit impacted them and some of them fell to the ground. Other signs of God's power were obvious for all to see.

My friend's wife apologised, assuming that he'd find the experience weird and off-putting. Far from it – he found it intriguing and was affected by the reality of God's power. This event turned out to be a key moment in his journey towards coming to know Jesus. Today he is now a pastor with a real hunger to see the power of the Spirit demonstrated.

We can make assumptions about peoples' reactions but my reflections on many stories like this lead me to believe that those who don't know Jesus are less likely to be repelled by demonstrations of God's power than by the expressions of hollow religion.

Another reason people reject Jesus is because of their experiences of judgmental Christians. This is another hallmark of hollow religion. Hollow religion breeds judgmentalism. Many genuine seekers have been put off following Jesus because of their painful past memories of being judged by Christians.

When people are given a hollow version of Christianity it inoculates them against the Gospel, causing them to miss profound life-changing encounters with God. This is tragic. When the Apostle Paul writes about conversion, he writes about the extraordinary transition from death to life which occurs at salvation. One example is in Ephesians 2:

"God, being rich in mercy, because of the great love with which he loved us, even when we were dead in our trespasses, made us alive together with Christ—by grace you have been saved — and raised us up with him and seated us with him in the heavenly places in Christ Jesus." (Ephesians 2:4-6)

In this brief passage Paul describes much of our story of redemption. Beginning with God's grace and love, Paul shows how God initiates our rescue, bringing life out of death. However, the story doesn't end just with being rescued. Paul shows how God lifts us up and seats us (notice present tense) with Christ in the heavenly realms. Not only does salvation bring about a transition from being dead sinners to fully alive children of God. It raises us up to the place where we are seated with authority and relationship with Him in heaven.

There is no greater transition which can happen to a person. It is like a pauper becoming a prince.

It breaks my heart that hollow religion leads people away from such a dramatic transformation.

All hollow religion offers is a set of principles and a collection of doctrines. It does not offer an encounter with Jesus and the beginning of an authentic relationship with Him. Remember what Jesus says in Matthew 23:15 about the Pharisees and their attempts at creating converts:

"Woe to you, scribes and Pharisees, hypocrites! For you travel across sea and land to make a single proselyte, and when he becomes a proselyte, you make him twice as much a child of hell as yourselves."

When a faith becomes institutional, then evangelism becomes more about joining a club or a movement than coming to know the Creator of the universe as Lord, friend and Saviour. Most of us see this at work in other parts of the Church but sometimes miss it when it manifests in our own church communities.

For example, a church or movement for renewal which carries a great deal of vision for reformation can be attractive to those with a passion for change. When hollow religion comes into play in this kind of context, their involvement can be driven primarily by their longing for change rather than by a personal relationship with Jesus.

Hollow religion bears the fruit of either repelling the lost (because of its emphasis on form rather than power) or attracting them to something other than a saving relationship with Jesus. People might join the club for a while but they will soon discover that what it prioritises does not fill the soul's longing for reconnection with the Father through Jesus.

A culture that is excited about knowing Jesus, willing to talk about relating to Him, seeing Him at work, opening hearts and sharing how He has brought people real life, will lead others into the same experience.

## The Fruit of Leadership

The enemy's strategy is to grow hollow religion in the Church by infecting its leaders. If leaders can be seduced away from Kingdom living into hollow religion, then whole churches can be hindered from advancing God's purposes on earth.

Leaders reproduce whatever motivates them. If leaders are breathing in the green mist of hollow religion, they reproduce hollow religion in all that they plant. They duplicate it in the life of the body they lead so that hollow religious worship and hollow religious evangelism become normal in the church.

Leaders who have become poisoned by hollow religion emphasize hard work and striving to keep up appearance and maintain reputation. Hollow leadership is built on human principles which are rooted in selfishness and personal gain. The fruit this produces is an emphasis on protecting those things which matter personally for the leader. Leaders in such contexts become self-protective and self-promoting rather than self-denying and self-sacrificial.

The typical fruit from this is controlling and ultimately abusive leadership – leadership in which people become slaves to the leader's vision and are exploited for the sake of the institution. Within this context, loving authority is replaced by control, gentle encouragement by pressure, healthy submission by coercion.

Kingdom leadership is the exact opposite. I love being around leaders who lead out of their own relationship with God, as disciples of Jesus. They lead with humility, love, honesty and joy. They are free to be themselves and be creative rather than feeling the need to fit into and preserve a mould. They are not preoccupied with defending themselves because they have found their security in being God's child. They are down-to-earth, accessible and refreshed by God and are then able to pour out love and blessing to those around them.

## The Fruit of Disagreement

Many years ago I worked in an open-plan office and one colleague and I regularly got into heated debates. If she held an opinion about a certain song, book, sports team, news item or brand of toothpaste, I would quickly consider all the arguments for the opposite opinion. If she argued that custard was yellow, I'd be passionate about it being orange.

One day in mid-debate (I've forgotten the topic, but the topic was usually irrelevant once we'd started) a picture came into my head. I was in a little castle with a catapult, hurling stones at her castle walls and she was in her castle, hurling stones at my walls.

I was defending my opinions and attacking everything she said. I had zero interest in listening to her, respecting her perspective or learning from her.

It suddenly occurred to me that I could walk out of my castle, attempt to meet her halfway and build a friendship with her. That would require humility and concession on my part so I hastily banished such ridiculous thoughts and got back to the argument! However, my approach changed that day. Later I confessed my destructive, defensive and proud attitude to God and promised to avoid getting stuck in my castle and just attacking others for the sake of it.

Hollow religion builds castles. It feeds on the desire for superiority and it excels in passing judgement on others. Hollow religion keeps Christianity firmly fixed within the castle walls of concepts and ideas. It only affects our intellects. Our hearts and spirits remain disengaged.

The fruit of this is debate, disagreement, and competition. As I have sought to rid my life of these ungodly fruits of hollow religion I have noticed how commonly accepted they have become within the Church and this grieves me.

Over recent years the growth of the Internet and social media has given more opportunity for virtual strangers to debate theology online without the social constraints of politeness or ongoing relationship. There's nothing sinful about followers of Jesus having different opinions and perspectives. It's what we do with them that matters. The hollow religious person is proud, believing their opinions are superior to others. He seeks to persuade others that they have to agree with them. The fruit of all this is division and factions within the body of Christ. This leads to the fragmentation of God's family. An enormous amount of time, energy and head space is then expended in competitive religious activity.

When God's children come together in humility to discuss, listen and learn, to hear what God has spoken to others, to build up not tear down, wonderful growth can happen.

Whilst attending a large conference, a friend invited me to join him for supper. Also included was a group of friends who were the leadership team of a large well-known church. I turned up, shy and intimidated by their status. My previous experience of situations like this told me that a group like this would have strong views and that I would be walking through a minefield. One articulated thought could trigger a strong opinionated reaction. I was nervous because they didn't know me and I didn't know the protocols.

My previous experience was no guide for what I encountered. Through the meal I felt valued. When I started a story no one interrupted but gave time for me to finish it. There was no cynicism or argumentativeness. There was no critical dismissal of the session of the conference that had taken place just before the meal. It was a stunning evening - encouraging and life-giving.

In 2 Corinthians 13:11 Paul writes:

"Aim for restoration, comfort one another, agree with one another, live in peace; and the God of love and peace will be with you."

The God of love promises His presence and peace when being in relationship is more important to us than being right.

## The Fruit of Denominationalism

In 1981 the great evangelical pioneer David Watson, wrote: "The existence of over 9000 Christian denominations throughout the world is an insult to Christ."[i]

Over thirty years on, a great deal has changed. The boundary lines on the denominational map have been blurred or shifted. My generation does not respect the same labels as previous generations. But the Body of Christ is still not a unified, loving family preferring one another in love. Jesus' prayer for oneness in John 17 hasn't yet been fully answered. There are still factions, denominations, tribes, traditions and movements that separate God's family. We judge one another by religious labels and external appearance. In all of this we show just how infected we have become by hollow religion. Hollow religion divides what God desires to bring together.

One of the hallmarks of the work of the Holy Spirit is the demolition of these barriers. Think of the way the Alpha Course has been embraced by all denominations. The Alpha Course – designed to lead seekers into a real experience and encounter with Jesus – is a course that was born of the Holy Spirit. People of every kind of denomination have seen the fruit in the masses of transformed lives when these courses have been held in their churches. This is the evidence that the Holy Spirit is at work. Not only is the Gospel preached and the Holy Spirit encountered. The family of God is united.

Hollow religion isolates but the Holy Spirit integrates.

## Pruning the Branches

When we start to recognise the rotten fruit of hollow religion and the damage it causes to the call on God's children to extend His kingdom, we then become intentional about pruning those branches which bear this kind of religious fruit. If God wants to prune those of us who are connected to the True Vine (Jesus), how much more does He want to prune those who are disconnected from the Vine because of hollow religion! Even when we bear good fruit, God still wants to prune us further.

That process of cutting off the branches of hollow religion isn't done through criticism, more debate or controlling those who are operating in such a mindset. It is done through humble repentance, through recognising where we have let hollow religion take root in our lives, and by turning back to obedient relationship with God. Jesus said in John 15:1-4:

"I am the true vine, and my Father is the vinedresser. Every branch in me that does not bear fruit he takes away, and every branch that does bear fruit he prunes, that it may bear more fruit. Already you are clean because of the word that I have spoken to you. Abide in me, and I in you. As the branch cannot bear fruit by itself, unless it abides in the vine, neither can you, unless you abide in me."

It's time for a radical pruning of the Vine.

It's time for hollow religion to be cut away.

Great productivity comes from great intimacy.

Genuine Christianity is relational not religious.

# 4

# A Great Awakening

Many of us have been rendered powerless in the Church as a result of opting for hollow religion. Is there any cure for this condition? The good news is that there is!

So how do we get out of the house of green mist and enter the Father's house, enjoying the breath and the life of heaven? The answer is we need to wake up, rise up and cough up. In later chapters we will also see that we need to look up.

Let's look at the first three in this chapter.

## Step 1: Wake Up

Jesus said in Mark 14:38, "Watch and pray that you may not enter into temptation. The spirit indeed is willing, but the flesh is weak." God wants us to wake up from the sleepy state caused by hollow religion.

Since God woke me up I've been so encouraged by the amazing ways I've seen Him waking others in the UK Church and around the world. It's truly time for the Church to experience an awakening!

Jesus described those who had died as "asleep" before waking them up. Lazarus is a good example. Jesus told his disciples that Lazarus was asleep, meaning dead. He then went and woke him up. He gave him back his life.

The Greek word used for "sleep" can be used figuratively to mean "dead" and is employed in this way in the New Testament.

If we believe that Ceri's dream described in the introduction is revelation from God (as I do), then we need to interpret it in the light of Scripture. The people in the house were asleep. At the same time they were in mortal danger. Had they remained asleep they would have died. All this goes to show the deadening effect of toxic religion.

In Isaiah 29 we read this:

"For the LORD has poured out upon you a spirit of deep sleep, and has closed your eyes (the prophets), and covered your heads (the seers). And the vision of all this has become to you like the words of a book that is sealed. When men give it to one who can read, saying, 'Read this,' he says, 'I cannot, for it is sealed.'" (Isaiah 29:10–11)

This spirit of stupor is directly linked in Isaiah 29.13 with the exercise of hollow religion:

"And the Lord said: 'Because this people draw near with their mouth and honour me with their lips, while their hearts are far from me, and their fear of me is a commandment taught by men.'" (Isaiah 29:13–14 ESV)

As so often with Old Testament prophesies, these words describe adverse circumstances as the result of the sovereignty of God. They are God's punishment for spiritual blindness. At the same time, they are often quickly followed up with words of hope for restoration:

"Therefore, behold, I will again do wonderful things with this people, with wonder upon wonder." (Isaiah 29:14 ESV)

"In that day the deaf shall hear the words of a book and out of their gloom and darkness the eyes of the blind shall see. The meek shall obtain fresh joy in the LORD, and the poor among mankind shall exult in the Holy One of Israel." (Isaiah 29:18–19 ESV)

These words leave us in little doubt: hollow religion causes us to become spiritually asleep. God wants to wake us up.

## The Drowsy Apostle

In Acts 10 Peter was praying on a roof top in Joppa. Luke describes what happened next:

"He fell into a trance and saw the heavens opened and something like a great sheet descending, being let down by its four corners upon the earth. In it were all kinds of animals and reptiles and birds of the air. And there came a voice to him: 'Rise, Peter; kill and eat.' But Peter said, 'By no means, Lord; for I have never eaten anything that is common or unclean.' And the voice came to him again a second time, 'What God has made clean, do not call common.'" (Acts 10:13–15)

Let's remember the context. Peter had to be persuaded by the Holy Spirit to take the Good News about Jesus to the Gentiles, to those who were ethnically different from him. In the end, he had to receive a powerful open vision before he would do what the Father wanted and move beyond his own people (the Jews) to those outside the Jewish fold.

This raises a big question. How open am I to the Holy Spirit giving me a radical paradigm shift in my thinking?

I believe that all prophetic revelation should be tested by Scripture. I believe the Bible is the inspired Word of God and our foundational authority for understanding God and His kingdom. Peter believed the same and yet his understanding of the Word was moulded more by tradition than by revelation. This is why the Holy Spirit sent him a supernatural vision that directly contradicted what he believed to be right. This open vision or trance presented him with a choice: to remain static by rigidly holding on to tradition, or to become dynamic and teachable, open to fresh revelation from God.

This wrestling between tradition and revelation goes on throughout the story. Peter visits Cornelius' household and explains that, according to his tradition, he "should" not eat with unclean Gentiles, but God has "shown me that I should not call any person common or unclean." He then boldly chooses to stay with them and share the Good News about Jesus. As he does the Holy Spirit falls on this Gentile household and they begin to speak in tongues and praise God.

The group who have travelled from Joppa with Peter – circumcised Jews – are amazed that God is choosing to pour out His Holy Spirit on unclean Gentiles. These events are outside their worldview, which revolved around the belief that God is the God of Abraham, Isaac and Jacob, the God of the Jews. For this God to pour out His Holy Spirit on Gentiles was shocking and hugely challenging. It presented them with a choice: to cling to their tradition or be open to the Holy Spirit expanding their understanding of God's ways.

In the first chapter of Acts Jesus had promised that His disciples would be His witnesses in Jerusalem, Judea, Samaria and to the ends of the earth.[i] In chapter ten, just before this story, Luke puts a marker in the ground, saying that the Church is established and growing in Judea, Galilee and Samaria. This becomes the gateway for the next phase of the story; the growth of the Church's witness to the ends of the earth. Acts 10 therefore describes a significant shift in the expansion of the kingdom.

I visited Israel a number of years ago and was privileged to be guided around the country by a man who had grown up in a highly respected and renowned strict Orthodox Jewish dynasty. Later in life he had come to know Jesus personally and his own story gave him fascinating insights into the interaction between Jewish beliefs and relationship with Jesus.

Our tour of the country began when he took us to Caesarea and, as we stood on the seaside Coliseum, said, "This is where it all began." I was startled that he placed such emphasis on a place far from Bethlehem, Nazareth, the Jordan and Jerusalem. But it was here that Cornelius and his household were saved and they were the first Gentiles to receive the Holy Spirit. This was only possible because Peter woke up to fresh revelation from God. He moved from hollow religion to fresh revelation.

## How Do We Wake Up?

Peter wakes up at two levels in Acts 10. He wakes up literally as he comes round from the effects of a Holy Spirit-inspired trance. He then wakes up spiritually as he comes round to the fresh revelation that God wants him to embrace. In fact, Peter's change of mind in Acts 10 is as radical, dramatic and history-making as the one that Cornelius and his household experience.

*All this goes to show that to wake up requires us to be flexible enough for God to change us.*

Peter's example shows that waking up from sleep in a literal sense has parallels with waking up in a spiritual sense. In the physical realm, we wake up from sleep when something in our immediate context changes – maybe a sudden noise, the switch of a light, or a rise in temperature. Any of these can cause us to wake up.

I believe God's preferred mode of speaking to us is through gentle whispers but when we're not listening He uses more drastic measures, including radical changes.

It is often in seasons of profound change that we are most open to hear God's revelation in those areas of our lives where we have become fixed and intransigent. God chose to take me to America to get my attention to see hollow religion in my life. I'm not sure I would have been so attentive if it had been part of normal life in the UK.

The ancient understanding of pilgrimage is significant here; it is often by removing ourselves from the comfort of our regular routines that we can position ourselves for fresh opportunities for God to speak to us, and experience those paradigm shifts that catapult us into the new normal of God's ways.

External changes are accordingly God's way of waking us up from hollow religion and introducing us to fresh revelation.

## The Power of Light

As in the natural, so it is in the spiritual. One external change can be sudden illumination. As the Apostle John writes: "God is light, and in him is no darkness at all. If we say we have fellowship with him while we walk in darkness, we lie and do not practice the truth. But if we walk in the light, as he is in the light, we have fellowship with one another, and the blood of Jesus his Son cleanses us from all sin" (1 John 1:5–7, ESV).

Although religion appears to be harsh on sin, immorality often accompanies it in discreet or hidden ways. If we hide from the light, we will continue in hollow religion. In fact hollow religion is often a very carefully constructed edifice we use to hide from the light.[ii]

Timothy Keller writes helpfully about this, distinguishing between the way in which religion bends our hearts while relationship melts them.

"Moralistic behaviour change bends a person into a different pattern through fear of consequences rather than melting a person into a new shape. But this does not work. If you try to bend a piece of metal without the softening effect of heat, it is likely to snap back to its former position. This is why we see people who try to change through moralistic behaviourism finding themselves repeatedly lapsing into sins they thought themselves incapable of committing."[iii]

When God's light breaks into the darker areas of our lives, it can wake us up, not just to our sin, but to the religious attitudes of self-righteousness, legalism and judgmentalism that have blinded us to the roots and reality of our sin.

Light is therefore one means of awakening.

## A Rousing Noise

I have a young family and it's usually my children who wake me up. There are two notable principles here. The first is that God chooses to speak through children and we do well to keep our ears open to them. Secondly one of the reasons children waken us is because they have felt needs. Being alert to the needs of those around us will wake up from hollow religion because hollow religion is ultimately self-serving.

Shouting can be effective too. I believe this is one of the responsibilities of those with the office of prophet in the church. As watchmen on the walls, they are called to shout the alarm when the people of God need to wake up.

When we read about the biblical prophets we can see that they were called to cry out to God's people: "A voice says, 'Cry!' And I said, 'What shall I cry?'"(Isaiah 40:6 ESV). Our responsibility is to open our ears when the prophets cry out to us.

Whenever I travel, I tend to take earplugs with me (particularly if there's an opportunity for a lie-in). Hollow religion tends to block our spiritual ears, causing us to sleep in when we should be awake, alert and active. Perhaps this is one reason why hollow religion is radically opposed to the prophetic. Those with religious power have often silenced prophets in ungodly ways. Silencing the prophets prevents us from being woken by God.

## Changes in Temperature

There are two ways that the temperature around us can wake us up - the first is in a spatial way, the second in a temporal way. Let's deal with spatial temperature changes first.

There have been times when I have visited a place and found levels of faith, joy, hope and love which are unusual. When we find ourselves suddenly immersed in a community which is living a more authentic expression of God's kingdom than we are accustomed to it can challenge or inspire us. This is because we have entered spaces where the spiritual temperature is a lot hotter than what we are used to. This can wake us up.

But then there are times as well as spaces that have the same effect. These are seasonal increases in temperature. Those who are open to the fresh revelation God wants to impart are particularly aware of these seasonal shifts. They are like the sons of Issachar who understood prophetically the times and the seasons.

We live in vastly changing times and God wants us to be alert to changes of temperature in both times as well as spaces. Moses, Samuel, David, Nehemiah, Jeremiah, Daniel, John the Baptist, Anna, Lydia and many others in the Bible were those who were alert to changes in God's seasons. Their sensitivity meant that God was able to use them and bring change through them.

## Hungry For God

There is perhaps one further factor to consider in addition to light, noise and temperature. This is more internal than external and it is hunger. Hunger can cause us to wake up.

Before we had children I was familiar with the battle between hunger and warmth, between the fridge and the bed. Many of those whom I am seeing waking out of hollow religion are those who are spiritually hungry. Hollow religion does not satisfy us. It makes our flesh comfortable but it cannot satisfy our spirits. It keeps us in a warm bed when we are called to open the cold fridge!

Our first step in breaking out of religion is therefore to wake up. As with salvation this awakening can be a sovereign act of God in our lives. The key our side is that once He begins to wake us up, we cooperate by agreeing to allow Him to bring change in our lives. Interestingly in Ceri's dream a number of people resisted waking up. They were warm and comfortable and wanted to roll over and tuck their heads under their duvets. That's a temptation I'm sure we can all recognise.

## Step 2: Rise up!

Having woken up, we have a choice to rise up or stay in bed. As children of God, our Father wants us to rise up to become who we truly are in Christ. Staying in the bed of hollow religion keeps us stuck in a false identity. It encourages us to be fake people - mask-wearers who have the appearance of godliness but not the reality. The process of waking up is the process of answering one of the most fundamental of all human questions: Who am I?

As I have tried to dig down to the theological roots of hollow religion one of the challenges I've had to face is whether the Bible defines us as fundamentally good or evil.

To summarise a lot of reading, listening, praying, talking and pondering I've come to a conclusion: we are both.

The Gospel is a story of our salvation, of God rescuing us. That story starts with God creating us in His image, of us rebelling and becoming sinful, worthless and dead. It then enters a redemptive phase when Jesus restores us to our original identity as "image bearers."

Hollow religion is often rooted in the chapters of the story in which we are degraded, worthless, lost in our failings and paralysed by our weaknesses.

The truth is we were all dead in our sins and we have all sinned and fallen short of God's glory. But the Gospel doesn't end there. Before the Fall we were created in God's image. In saving and restoring us as new creations, God is restoring us to the glory we once had.

*While our sin and its deathly influence might wake us up, it is the truth of how God sees us that compels us to rise up.*

When we realise who we are as royal children of God, then it gives us a reason to rise up from our beds. We realise that sleeping in a mist of toxic green gas is not something that befits those who are the royally adopted sons and daughters of the High King of Heaven!

Believing God's truth about our identity therefore motivates and empowers us to rise up out of hollow religion. As we wonder at the truth that He loves us, He values us, He respects us, He includes us, He welcomes us into His presence, He has created us on purpose and invites us to play a role in the family business - that's something to get out of bed for.

Recognising who we are then leads us to understand what we are called to do. It causes us to recognise our responsibility in the family business. This again is something to get up for.

Maturity involves recognizing and embracing the responsibility given to us by our Father. We then get out of our religious beds not for selfish reasons but to be a blessing to others.

As a church leader, I am so encouraged when I see people grasp hold of this truth. When someone is locked into hollow religion, their primary concern is how their behaviour impacts themselves. Hollow religion causes us to become essentially self-preoccupied. If my responsibility is to earn God's favour, do the right thing, and attempt to save myself, then my actions are self-serving, ultimately impacting me.

Once we live in the truth that God loves us unconditionally, accepts us as we are and has already saved us, then our actions of service, worship or ministry aren't motivated by self-interest but by the desire to give what we have to others.

*Remaining in hollow religion will not change the world but accepting your identity and responsibility as a child of God will bring heaven to earth.*

For this to happen, we will need non-religious pastors in God's Church!

We have seen how it is often the prophets who wake us up. I believe it is the role of pastoral fathers and mothers to raise us up. The role of parents is to speak into their children's lives, to nurture, encourage and affirm them. As pastors turn from hollow religion they turn from being controlling leaders to being releasing parents. They change from judging their flock to seeing them as children of God, with value and responsibility in the family business. This in turn enables them to speak with such motivating love that their people rise up with fresh dynamic, creative initiatives.

## Step 3: Cough Up!

Just to put you at your ease, this section isn't about tithing. It's about repentance!

Many of us have emotional responses to almost everything in life. These responses can be huge, minimal, buried, disproportionate, surprising, irrational, inexplicable and many more things besides. But whether it's to a type of car or a brand of toothpaste, or an idea or a person, at some level we all respond emotionally.

Advertisers understand this. They use images, colour schemes, type fonts, information layout, to encourage us to recognise their brand, to respond warmly, and to buy their products.

The same is true in relationships. We need to be honest here. We are attracted towards some people (not necessarily in a romantic or sexual way) and have negative emotional responses to others. These can, of course, fluctuate. Recognising this enables us to grow in maturity in our relationships and not reject, avoid or inappropriately rush to people, based on emotional triggers.

I believe the same principle applies to biblical truths and concepts. Those of us who preach intuitively know this. We can stir a crowd and raise an atmosphere very positively (and not necessarily manipulatively) by referring to exciting kingdom ideas such as joy, love, hope, healing, and salvation. In certain contexts, other keywords function as positive emotional triggers. In one church the word "truth" excites the majority; in another, it might be the word "miracles"; in another, "justice".

I developed a simple exercise with our staff team to test this out using a system of smiley faces and sad faces. I wrote a list of concepts relating to theological truths or aspects of church life and asked them to give an immediate emotional response (without taking the time for a considered thinking approach), by ticking a box in the smiley faced column or the sad faced column. The rules were simple; there would be no need to defend or justify our answers, just give our immediate feelings about the concept. I've filled in the first few on the response sheet as an example. Please fill in the second half (use a pencil in case you lend the book to someone else one day!)

|  | ☺ | ☹ |
|---|---|---|
| Love | ✓ | |
| Social justice | ✓ | |
| Evangelism | | ✓ |
| Tithing | | ✓ |
| Intercession | ✓ | |
| Early morning prayer meetings | | ✓ |
| Generosity | | |
| Worship | | |
| Authority | | |
| Spiritual warfare | | |
| Servanthood | | |
| Hope | | |
| Salvation | | |
| Sacrificial giving | | |
| Ministry to the poor | | |
| Repentance | | |
| Welcoming newcomers to church | | |
| Formal worship | | |

There are two purposes here. The first is to be honest and recognise how much our emotions play a part in our judgments and how this can affect our obedience (all of the above are either modelled or commanded in Scripture). The second is to recognise that there are some aspects of the kingdom of God to which we can react with negative emotion. This can become dangerous when we act upon that emotion and then justify our actions with a dismissal of or an argument against the value in question.

## The "R" Word

An area where this is particularly prevalent is repentance. In some places even talking about this gift from God is seen as a taboo. There all sorts of imbalanced teachings can emerge, designed to marginalise the importance of this foundational aspect of the disciple's walk with Jesus. When this happens it is often our emotional triggers that are to blame. They can cause us to associate a positive biblical concept with a negative feeling or experience. Add to this the fact that we live in a culture that runs from pain and you have the cocktail for moral disaster.

The biblical view of repentance is wholly different from what much of the 21st Century Western church feels about it. Paul the Apostle spoke about the kindness of God leading us to repentance (Romans 2:4) yet many of us associate repentance with His sternness. This is because hollow religion specialises in sternness while the culture of heaven specialises in kindness. Taking our simple model of smiley and sad faces, for many of us experience a profound tension when we hear this verse. Our faces smile when they are presented with the word "kindness" and look sad at the word "repentance."

Some translations pick up on this tension. The NIV says: "not realising that God's kindness is *intended* to lead you to repentance." The Message paraphrase says: "God is kind, *but he's not soft*. In kindness he takes us firmly by the hand and leads us into a radical life-change."

These versions contain an implicit expectation that repentance is hard and painful. In a culture that anaesthetises itself from all forms of pain, some readers might react by saying, "If repentance equals pain, let's bin repentance." But what the verse actually teaches is that repentance is a gift from our heavenly Father and an expression of His kindness. It reveals that God, our loving heavenly Father, doesn't want us to avoid repentance in order to make discipleship more palatable, nor does He wants us to become stuck in an endless cycle of agonising self-condemnation because religion says "it's good for us." He wants us to understand repentance from heaven's point of view, and that means positively. The Greek word metanoia, translated "repentance", literally means a change of mind and a change of direction. I remember clearly over twenty years ago the evangelist and ex-footballer Graham Daniels speaking at my school, explaining the Gospel and using a simple illustration to describe repentance.

He walked towards one side of the stage, symbolising walking away from God. He then turned around and walked back across the stage in the other direction, towards God. That's repentance: changing your mind and turning around, back into relationship with God. Although we don't always like change, turning back to a perfect, loving Father is a good thing!

When we turn back to relationship with our Father, we turn away from the enemy's lies. Repentance therefore involves spiritual warfare. The enemy is only allowed the amount of influence we give him. The devil and the demonic realm have all been defeated by the crucifixion and resurrection of the Son of God. When we believe the enemies' lies, we open ourselves up to their influence. If we are walking away from God and his loving truth, then we are walking towards the voice of the enemy and hearing his lies. The deception we hear will depend on the direction we choose.

When we repent we remove the influence of the demonic lies

in our lives. Part of coughing up means choosing to rebuke the enemy and doing what Jesus did, commanding lying spirits from having any further influence. I have seen this simple action of repentance and rebuking bear extraordinary fruit in my own life and the lives of many others.

## Life-Changing Kindness

A few years ago my wife and I were praying with a young man. In the model of prayer ministry we were following, the typical next step was to ask the Holy Spirit what was blocking his relationship with God. But I intuitively sensed the Holy Spirit leading us on another route. I prayed, "Lord, what is the question here?" What I sensed the Holy Spirit say was this: "Ask him who told him that he doesn't exist?"

I hesitantly shared it with him. He went white as a sheet and through tears shared he had been born as the result of an adulterous relationship. His father had stayed in touch with his mother throughout his life but he had never told his wife and family that he had another son. This man's whole life had been lived under the cloud of the lies of his father. He shared how he attended his father's funeral pretending to be a stranger, meeting his half-brothers and sisters, unable to explain to them who he was. He had battled with a deep sense of shame and anonymity all his life and what kept him distant from God was the sense that he was illegitimate and didn't really exist or matter.

That whole sense of shame and anonymity was based on a lie. When God revealed that lie and we replaced it with the truth, rebuking the enemy in the process, the freedom was dramatic. An hour after the prayer time I stood near him in worship. His face was transformed. He looked like a completely different person. He seemed so much more alive, so much lighter and freer to be himself. It was one of the most moving and powerful transformations I have ever seen.

Repentance is accordingly a life-changing encounter with God's kindness, leading us from the enemy's lies (which cause us to fall asleep) to the Father's truths (which cause us to wake up and truly live).

## Focusing on Pain

In spite of this, it is still possible for people to turn repentance from a real experience into a religious act. It's even possible for us to become "professional repenters" – something that should be an obvious contradiction in terms. When this happens we have accepted an understanding of repentance based on the enemy's lies. This leads us in turn to inhale the green mist of toxic and hollow religion.

This happened to me. One day I caught myself attempting to say the words of repentance as I cycled into work, whilst also concentrating on the traffic and getting angry with the 4x4s blocking the cycle lane! I was saying the right words, but my heart was far from God.

*Repentance is supposed to be real not religious.*

We need to understand just how powerful repentance is when it's real. Repentance is a radical transition from coming out of agreement with enemy lies and entering into agreement with God. Repentance is accordingly a legal transaction. By switching changing our agreement, we determine who has influence over us in the heavenly realms.

For many Christians from a variety of church backgrounds, repentance has a sad face trigger because it is associated with the emotional pain which accompanies recognition of sin. This can be a healthy part of the repentance process – when we see how our choices, beliefs, actions and habits have separated us from our loving Father and from others. This can stir up emotions of regret and shame. Broken relationships hurt, both with the Father and with others.

But repentance is not measured by the level of emotion accompanying it. In 2 Corinthians 7 Paul writes:

"For even if I made you grieve with my letter, I do not regret it — though I did regret it, for I see that that letter grieved you, though only for a while. As it is, I rejoice, not because you were grieved, but because you were grieved into repenting. For you felt a godly grief, so that you suffered no loss through us. *For godly grief produces a repentance that leads to salvation without regret, whereas worldly grief produces death.* For see what earnestness this godly grief has produced in you, but also what eagerness to clear yourselves, what indignation, what fear, what longing, what zeal, what punishment! At every point you have proved yourselves innocent in the matter." (2 Corinthians 7:8–11)

Throughout 2 Corinthians Paul writes with a remarkable combination of tender humility and apostolic authority, seeking reconciliation with those members of the church in Corinth who have broken their relationship with him.

In this passage, Paul refers back to a previous letter which had grieved them but rejoices that their grief caused them to repent. He then contrasts godly grief, which leads to repentance, with ungodly sorrow that leads to death.

Living in a fallen world involves dealing with our sin, recognising its roots, identifying the lies we have believed and acknowledging the consequences. This can be painful which is why Paul talks about godly grief. Godly grief is focussed on the pain that our sin has caused to God our Father. Worldly grief focuses on the pain we have caused to ourselves. True repentance is turning from being self-centred to God-centred.

## It's Time to Cough Up

Once we have obeyed the call to wake up and rise up, we need to cough up. But coughing up should never become a religious ritual. It should always be a case of coming home to the Father's arms and the Father's house, replacing the green mist of hollow religion for the warm breath of heaven.

Repentance is coughing up the green gas of the lies that rob us of our intimacy with God. For someone to clear their lungs they need to relax and inhale fresh air and exhale the toxic gas. Becoming absorbed with how awful the gas is and the agony it has caused us is not repentance. Focusing on regrets and reliving them is not repentance either. To borrow a line from one of my favourite worship songs, "I don't have time to maintain these regrets when I think about the way He loves us."[iv]

The difference between the condemnation of the accuser and the conviction of the Holy Spirit is this: the accuser grabs the back of our head and rubs our nose in the mess of our sin. The Holy Spirit takes hold of our face and lifts us up and above the mess of our sin to meet with Jesus face-to-face.

### Notes

i. Acts 1.8

ii. This is explored powerfully in Ch16 of Philip Yancey's *What's So Amazing About Grace?*

iii. Timothy Keller, *Center Church,* p67.

iv. John Mark McMillan, *How He Loves Us.*

# 5

# God is Relational

Having woken up, risen up, coughed up our fourth action is to look up.

God reveals Himself in the Bible as Father, Son and Holy Spirit. Intimate communion with all three members of the Trinity is the opposite of living in hollow religion.

Hollow religion is attempting to please or appease God whilst living at a distance from Him.

Genuine relationship means being reconciled to the Father, Son and Holy Spirit and living as the friends of God.

## I Am Your Father!

God is a loving Father. Jesus regularly spoke of God in this way, as His father and our Father. In John 1:12, as the great prologue to John's Gospel reaches its climax, John proclaims: "But to all who did receive him, who believed in his name, he gave the right to become children of God." We are God's adopted children and He is our affectionate Father. This is a foundational truth, a solid rock on which we can build our lives. Everything needs to be interpreted in light of this glorious revelation. Our Father loves us and delights in us. He created us in His image. He knitted us together in our mother's womb. He called us His children and rejoices over us with singing.

As Father, God regularly takes opportunities to show me how much He loves me through the love I have for my boys. This afternoon was beautifully sunny and I sat in dappled sunshine under the branches of a willow tree in our garden. After school my three-year-old son popped out into the garden, walked over to the trampoline, carefully unzipped it and bounced a few times in utter freedom and abandonment. He was totally unaware that his dad was watching him. I had tears of joy and delight running down my face, seeing him enjoy himself.

At moments like these the Holy Spirit always reminds me, "That's how the Father looks at you and what you're doing." When God watches you, He's not looking out for your sin in order to catch you out or correct you. He's enjoying who you are and celebrating how much He loves you.

Many of us recognise that our own experience of being fathered shapes our understanding of fatherhood in both conscious and subconscious ways. The way our fathers, or father-figures, treated us in childhood will shape what we believe fathering to be, both good and bad. We can't avoid this. The most honest thing to do is recognise it, submit it to our heavenly Father and ask the Holy Spirit to expand and realign our understanding of fathering, so that it becomes one with the true character of God, rather than shaped by poor earthly fathers.

As we read the Bible, it's essential that we ask the Father to reveal more of His true nature to us so that this overrides whatever we already believe about fathering. I have often fallen into the trap of doing it the other way around – bringing my preconceptions about fatherhood and then reading them into what the Bible teaches about God the Father. This is a lifelong process. The goal is not to have a perfect theology of the Father but rather a heart-relationship with Him in which true fatherhood is understood through His demonstrations of love.

My own experience of being fathered was a mainly positive one. I grew up in a secure home with loving parents and a dad who understood the importance of loving and nurturing his children. However, my dad died suddenly when I was 27 years old. As I sat in the taxi rushing to the hospital I was reminded of a story a friend told me when he was in a very similar circumstance, on the day his father died. As he sat on the plane from Edinburgh to London God spoke to him from Psalm 2:7 (NIV): "You are my son, today I have become your father."

As soon as I remembered this, those exact words landed in my heart so powerfully that they still remain there to this day. I knew that day my dad would die and those words of comfort from my Heavenly Father gave me a brand new relationship with Him - one that has been a life-giving reality ever since.

Five years later I was standing at the front of our church. It was the first Sunday of our senior pastor's sabbatical and I was in sole charge. It was also Father's Day, something I had previously found painful because of my dad's death. As I stood worshipping and leading, I looked up to heaven and sensed the presence of my Heavenly Father as close and overwhelmingly loving as I've ever known Him. The phrase that came to mind was, "This is what open heaven is like." I knew then there are absolutely no layers between my heavenly Father and me. I have direct access to Him. Suddenly leading a church seemed a whole lot easier!

## The Father's Welcome

This is God's design for His children: to build the family business in whatever sphere He calls us to and to do so with direct access to Him.

I love the story about the high-powered politicians being confused at the sound of a young child playing in the Oval Office in the White House. They discovered it was the President's son. That boy had access to the most powerful office in the world and was free to play there – free to talk to his father in a way that no one on the president's staff was permitted to. This is our destiny too as the children of God - we are not meant to experience fearful distance but playful proximity.

Here are two Scriptures to encourage us:

"Let us then with confidence draw near to the throne of grace, that we may receive mercy and find grace to help in time of need." (Hebrews 4:16)

"Therefore, brothers, since we have confidence to enter the holy places by the blood of Jesus, by the new and living way that he opened for us through the curtain, that is, through his flesh, and since we have a great priest over the house of God, let us draw near with a true heart in full assurance of faith, with our hearts sprinkled clean from an evil conscience and our bodies washed with pure water." (Hebrews 10:19–22)

The more we absorb the truth that God the Father invites us to come unashamedly and freely into His Presence, the more hollow religion is swept away because hollow religion is built on the lie that we are distant from God.

All religious activity and thinking stems from that lie. The great truth that we are welcomed by our Heavenly Father dissolves hollow religion in our lives.

## The Religious Dam

I was recently privileged to meet William P. Young (author of

The Shack). In a question-and-answer session with some church leaders he shared a powerful vision which his friend C. Baxter Kruger had shared with him of a beaver dam. This is how Baxter describes the vision:

"The vision that the Lord gave to me was of a vast dam that could stop up a river as great as the Mississippi. I believe this was intended to help me understand what has happened in the Western tradition. The two huge, Redwood trees at the bottom, crossing one another were the lie of human separation from the Father, Son and Spirit, and the lie that the Father is not fundamentally good, and thus cannot be trusted. All the other trees and rocks and limbs and mud making up the dam were connected to these core lies."[i]

This vision captures the very heart of what this book is really about. I believe God is saying that it's time to demolish that dam. Each of us can demolish it in our own lives by seeking to pull down every form of the lie that we cannot trust the Father.

The morning after I met William P. Young I woke up suddenly at 5.40am with a question bursting in my head: "What are the best tools to help us demolish the lie that we are distant from God?" I was camping with my whole family in a trailer tent. I crept out carefully (not wanting to wake up over-tired small children at that time of day) and walked to the toilet block. As I made my way there I had an extraordinary sense of God walking alongside me through the campsite. I could feel His heart and He let me experience some of His pain. The only way I can describe what I felt was that as we walked between the tents of sleeping people the Father was saying to me: "I long to be close to them but they keep me at arm's distance because they don't trust that I'm good." I returned to bed buzzing with Holy Spirit energy and lay there praying. For some reason I asked the Lord why He'd woken me at 5.40am (I had noticed that I'd been waking at that time quite regularly that summer). He prompted me to read John 5:40: "Yet you refuse to come to me that you may have life." This comes from a lengthy speech by Jesus addressed to the religious leaders in Jerusalem who were persecuting Him for healing a man on the Sabbath.

When we live at a distance from the Father, when we refuse to trust Him, we resort to hollow religion to fill the gap. But Jesus came to reconcile us with His Father. He came to bridge the great divide between us and the Father. He came to provide atonement, that is to say at-one-ment, between estranged orphans and a perfect Father in heaven. This is the Good News! The Gospel is at least in part the message that the Father himself loves us dearly (John 16:27) and has bridged the gap between Him and us. What could be more amazing than that?

## The Perfect Father

The Lord's Prayer gives us some key biblical principles for how we relate to our Heavenly Father.

*Our Father in Heaven...*

Above all else, Jesus encouraged his disciples to address God as Abba Father – our loving, Heavenly Papa or Dad. The word translated "Father" denotes respect but it also denotes intimacy and affection. Isn't it amazing how people say these words so religiously? Yet the very start of the prayer, "Our Dad who is in Heaven", is the very opposite of religion. It is relationship and reality! When people learn how to say these words with feeling, then the green mist of hollow religion is immediately expelled.

*Hallowed be your name...*

In recent years the Western Church has been waking up to the importance of honour. This is certainly true in my life. However, giving honour is profoundly counter-cultural in the UK.

The day after writing part of this book, I went to my son's end-of-year school assembly. My head was full of thoughts about hollow religion, about form without power, about the emptiness of Christianity without tangible clear expressions of the Holy Spirit's power in signs, wonders, miracles and the use of the gifts of the Spirit. In that assembly the children sang Christian hymns and prayed prayers in a formal, structured setting, with a number of people joining in who would not describe themselves as Christians.

Although so much of the event seemed to parallel what I had been thinking about hollow religion, and be the furthest remove from the experience of worship I had been imagining, I had to recognise that what was going on was profoundly good. The values and truths these children were learning are essential if they are to grow into mature and godly children of God.

Then the main event of the assembly happened. Each of the leavers (eleven-year-olds) stood on the stage as the head teacher gave a brief speech honouring their character and talents. Shivers went down my spine and my eyes leaked … a lot! I was immediately aware of a sense of the Father's pleasure; He had hijacked my emotions to ensure I learned from it (He is allowed to do that; He's in charge!)

Honour matters to God. I believe He really enjoys us celebrating one another. Jesus told his disciples to honour the Father's name when they prayed. That means valuing, esteeming and exalting the name that Jesus revealed about God – that He is our loving, adoring Heavenly Abba Father!

## A Culture of Dishonour
In the Bible, children are exhorted to honour their parents. This

is such a significant part of Kingdom culture that God included it in the Ten Commandments. Just as we are called to honour our earthly parents, so we are commanded to honour our Father who is in heaven. We are called to honour His name – the unique name that Jesus brought from heaven to earth, the name Father. What a sad fact of life it is that in so many places honouring our Heavenly Father and earthly fathers is so rare.

In the summer of 2011, quite suddenly riots broke out in parts of London and then spread like a wildfire into other towns and cities in the UK. For many it was a shock, a moment of realisation of the depth of malaise in our nation. Chief Rabbi Lord Sacks commented: "There are moments in the history of any civilisation when it catches a glimpse of the state of its soul. We have just seen ours, and it has not been a pleasant sight."[ii] Two months earlier, Prime Minister David Cameron had written an article in a national newspaper about the essential importance of fathers embracing the responsibility to invest in their children's lives. When the riots hit, Cameron identified fatherlessness as one of the main causes.

One of the hallmarks of a collapsing society is a lack of honour for parents. The final words of the Old Testament are: "Behold, I will send you Elijah the prophet before the great and awesome day of the LORD comes. And he will turn the hearts of fathers to their children and the hearts of children to their fathers, lest I come and strike the land with a decree of utter destruction" (Malachi 4:5–6). This prophecy is very significant not only for the great purposes of God but for our own times.

In the church where I grew up, as well as in my family, this was a favourite passage of Scripture but I never understood why. More recently I have realised that God has designed His Kingdom to be a family. When He speaks through His Word, this is the wisdom

He gives as Father to us His children.

Children don't listen to their parent's advice when there is broken relationship, when trust has been shattered. If the fathers' hearts are turned away from their children – if they are distracted by work, or other interests or even adulterous relationships – then that relationship of trust, that bond is broken.

God's great Kingdom is built on healthy family relationships. Those relationships are the channels by which God's wisdom can pass from one generation to the next. That is crucial in establishing healthy society. This means that reconciliation between parents and children is central to His purposes on the earth.

## Looking Up in Prayer

The whole point about the opening of the Lord's Prayer is this: Jesus wants us to look up as God's children into the affectionate face of our Father in Heaven. He wants us to join with all the other royally adopted sons and daughters of God across the earth and call God, "Dad, Dearest Father, and Pops." He wants us to use that special name for God and in doing so destroy the lie that God is remote, unmoved, dispassionate, aloof, uncaring and punitive. God is the most loving Father in the universe. Even the best dads on earth are only a pale reflection.

Jesus made this the top priority in His teaching on prayer. We need to learn how to "relate up". We should be passionate about intimacy with the Father and about the freedom of access we have into His presence. We should experience His tenderness, His grace, His forgiveness, His kindness, and His joy every day.

All this shows that learning to honour Him does not mean relating in toxic fear, as though He was far away. It is learning to celebrate who He is through praise and worship, honouring His generosity through regularly saying "Thank you" and submitting to Him through obedience at every level.

This is profoundly unreligious because honouring God comes down to a baseline of living for Him and not for ourselves. Hollow religion causes us to be self-serving. It teaches us to become experts and connoisseurs of praise and in the process to move to ideas about worship rather than the experience of worship. The truth is that my personal preference for worship styles is irrelevant. Worship is to God, about God and for God. Worship is us feeling so blessed as His children that as we worship Him and give Him undivided attention He graciously scoops us up into His arms and gives us the treat of enjoying His embrace. As we honour Him, He reciprocates by honouring us! That is amazing grace indeed!

## Heaven on Earth

As we saw in an earlier chapter, separation from God started with the question, "Did God really say?" This question implied that God is distant and can't be trusted. Questioning what God has said is a strategy designed to keep us isolated from God. Honouring Him restores in us the truth that God is good and can be trusted. As we honour God in words and songs, we witness to the truth that God is good. We remind each other that there is no need for us to be isolated from Him because He is a good Father who likes to be with His kids.

This is something Jesus points to in the next clause of the Lord's Prayer:

*Your kingdom come, your will be done, on earth as it is in heaven...*

Another truth which God is revealing again to the contemporary church is that heaven isn't just a far-off place we go to when we die but the realm in which He lives in permanent glorious majesty, a realm that comes to us while we are alive.

The Father likes to be where His children are and so Jesus urges us to pray that heaven will come to earth.

In Genesis 3, when Adam and Eve hide because of their shame, God comes looking for them and calls out to them. When we were far away from God, He came to earth as a man to reconcile us to Himself. He came to seek, find and embrace His lost and orphaned children.

This is the Father's heart. "God will not take away life, and he devises means so that the banished one will not remain an outcast" (2 Samuel 14:14). The Bible is the story of God seeking out His lost children and reconciling us to Himself and then including us in the family business of helping others to seek and find their way back into His arms.

## Long Distance

For the whole time my wife and I were going out, we rarely went out with each other because I lived on a different continent from her and then a different city. We had to communicate from far away rather than close by.

Long distance relationships aren't much fun. Communication can become more about maintaining the relationship than growing and deepening love. It was wonderful when we finally married and could live together as a couple; our relationship became so much more enjoyable when we could communicate face-to-face.

This is a helpful analogy. The purpose of Jesus' reconciling death was that we experience God's presence. God wants us to experience and cultivate a growing, close relationship with Him. He wants that to develop through us not only praying, "Our Father in heaven," but also "let heaven come to earth."

One of my favourite quotes about religion comes from one of my greatest heroes, Bono (lead singer of the band U2): "Religion is the thing when God, like Elvis, has left the building. But when God is in the house, you get something else."

Given that God loves to be with His children and we are transformed and become alive in His presence a burning question for me has been this: What is it that causes us to feel that God is far away?

As a child I was taught this: "If God feels far off, guess who has moved." The Bible reveals a God who is consistently longing for relationship with His children. There are only very rare occasions when He separates Himself from us and these are for specific reasons.

In Exodus 33, God is so angered by the Israelites' worship of the golden calf that He chooses to separate Himself from them. "I will not go up among you, lest I consume you on the way, for you are a stiff-necked people" (Exodus 33:3). God distances Himself for the people's protection here.

In the 6th century BC, many centuries later, the people of God are sent into exile in Babylon. There they lament, homesick for Jerusalem, the Temple and the presence of the Lord. Scriptures such as Psalm 74 express the pain of separation from God. The prophets, such as Jeremiah and Ezekiel, bring a theological understanding of this separation, saying that it is a fulfilment of the promise of the Covenant, that if the people rebelled against God, then disaster would come – the greatest disaster being the loss of His presence.

Today we live under the New Covenant. Jesus' death tore apart the curtain in the Temple symbolising separation from God. The Holy Spirit has been poured out on all flesh; relationship with Him is available for all. "For I am sure that neither death nor life, nor angels nor rulers, nor things present nor things to come, nor powers, nor height nor depth, nor anything else in all creation, will be able to separate us from the love of God in Christ Jesus our Lord" (Romans 8:38–39).

## Rediscovering the Father

There are a number of reasons why we back away from God's presence: we may be unaware that He invites us; we may be ashamed of our sin, afraid of punishment; or we may be consumed with our own lives and preoccupations and ignore Him.

One of the most common reasons for avoiding God's presence is fear. Now there is both a healthy and an unhealthy fear of God. In the Bible we hear of "the fear of the Lord" – an awe, wonder and recognition of His greatness which causes us to honour and worship Him. But there is also an unhealthy fear of God, based on the lie that He is angry, harsh, critical or disinterested.

There are two further fears related to this unhealthy fear – the fear of punishment and the fear of rejection. There are no grounds for us to have or to hold onto these fears. So often they relate not to good theology but to bad experiences of being fathered. Harsh, punitive, abusive fathers, or absent, disinterested, apathetic fathers, sow an expectation into our hearts that God will reject and punish us harshly.

One powerful way of removing this harmful perspective is through helping people engage with their imagination, under the direction of the Holy Spirit.

Let me give one example, from many, of how I have seen God heal and restore people in this way.

I was praying with a young woman who struggled with a sense of legalism, religion and acknowledged distance from God. She struggled to feel forgiven by God yet she was a delightful girl, a

Christian leader with a mature understanding of the Gospel and a good grasp of God's character.

I asked her to close her eyes. We invited the Holy Spirit to come and we bound in Jesus' name all lying spirits from having any influence on our time of prayer. I then asked her to imagine herself standing at the doorway to God the Father's study and describe to me what she saw.

She said that she could see herself as a small girl knocking on the study door. There was no reply. She knocked again but again there was no reply. I encouraged her to push through the door and see what was inside. As she walked in she could see a man at the far end of a very long room sat at a desk.

I was surprised by this. Usually when I do this exercise with people they quickly have an encounter with God the Father, welcoming them into the room with love. In her case it was quite different. The man she saw didn't even look up from his newspaper or acknowledge that she was there.

We paused and I asked her about her own father. It turned out that the picture was typical of how he had related to her – distant and preoccupied.

I encouraged her to forgive her father, repent of believing the lie that God is like him and ask God to replace that lie with the truth. She did this. Then when she closed her eyes again, she was outside the same door. As she knocked on the door, Jesus immediately opened it for her and welcomed her in. This time the scene was totally different. In her imagination she saw a beautiful sunlit garden, into which Jesus beckoned her. She then described to me how she and Jesus were sitting on a low wall, dangling their toes into some water, simply hanging out.

As we finished her whole demeanour and joy levels were transformed. I prayed that she would come to encounter the

Father in the same way that she had encountered Jesus because Jesus said "I and the Father are one" (John 10:30).

I have prayed with dozens of people in this way and seen many encounters like this. They have allowed people to relate to God with fresh and non-religious intimacy.

Rediscovering the Father's love can often involve a crisis-event like this. But we should not forget that there is a process too. For me there's always the ongoing choice to believe the truth that the Father accepts me as forgiven, rather than rejects me for being sinful. As I choose to believe this truth and renounce the lie, I break out of the cycle of condemnation and into God's presence so much more quickly.

## The Father Who Provides

*Give us today our daily bread...*

Good fathers like to provide for their children and the same is true of God. One of the Hebrew names for God in the Old Testament is Jehovah Jireh, meaning "God who provides."

"Every good gift and every perfect gift is from above, coming down from the Father of lights with whom there is no variation or shadow due to change." (James 1:17)

Knowing Abba Father as our reliable provider demolishes two characteristics of hollow religion. The first is trying to earn God's favour as wages, as opposed to receiving it as our inheritance.

In Luke 15 Jesus tells the moving story of a loving father, a prodigal younger son and an indignant older son. The story concludes with the father saying to the older son: "Son, you are always with me and all that is mine is yours." (Luke 15.31)

This older brother provides a poignant picture of hollow religion. He's jealous and resentful, proud and judgemental and he's missed the fact that he has free access to the father's resources because of his position not his performance. The older brother completely fails to see this, which is why he cries, "Look, these many years I have served you, and I have never disobeyed your command, yet you never gave me a young goat, that I might celebrate with my friends" (Luke 15:29). This son was expecting his father to give him a reward for his hard work. The father's mindset was totally different: "All that is mine is yours."

We have access to all of heaven's resources on the basis of our position as adopted daughters and sons, not on the basis of our performance. This is why Jesus says, "so that whatever you ask the Father in my name, he may give it to you" (John 15:16).

The key principle here is that of inheritance. Our loving Heavenly Father has so much more for us than we could ever ask or imagine. This is why Paul bursts into gratitude at the start of his letter to the Ephesians:

"Blessed be the God and Father of our Lord Jesus Christ, who has blessed us in Christ with every spiritual blessing in the heavenly places, even as he chose us in him before the foundation of the world." (Ephesians 1:3-4)

Paul fully realises that "In him we have obtained an inheritance" (Ephesians 1:11). This is why he prays, "May you be strengthened with all power according to his glorious might, for all endurance and patience with joy, giving thanks to the Father who has qualified you to share in the inheritance of the saints in light" (Colossians 1:11-12).

Here are some other Scriptures about inheritance:

"According to his great mercy he has caused us to be born again to a living hope through the resurrection of Jesus Christ from the dead, to an inheritance that is imperishable, undefiled and unfading." (1 Peter 1:3-4)

"For the wages of sin is death, but the free gift of God is eternal life in Christ Jesus our Lord." (Romans 6.23)

We don't work for God's favour; we work from God's favour.

When we live as orphans we try to earn God's favour and store up for ourselves whatever we feel we need to survive. We might try and gain knowledge, or wealth or influence. We might see prayer as 'putting in the hours', to store up favour or blessing. This religious approach to God often leads to jealousy of those who have more than us.

In the final part of the parable, we see from the reaction of the older brother that he has been living with a 'wages mindset' and this makes him jealous and judgemental. A great deal of religious criticism is rooted not in a righteous reaction to injustice but in sibling rivalry. The same Heavenly Father who says to the older brother, "Son, you are always with me, and all that is mine is yours," calls us all to believe that we are His children and to live in that truth. When we do it releases us to enjoy and not criticise the blessings that others receive.

Knowing God as a generous, loving provider demolishes one feature of hollow religion, which is our attempt to earn God's wages, rather than living in our inheritance.

It also demolishes another characteristic of hollow religion, which is the tendency to become greedy for things that are externally impressive, believing that they are the true indicators of value.

This can happen when we invest heavily in external rather than internal factors, in the things that are seen rather than unseen. When we believe that impressive buildings, music or presentations will bring heaven to earth we become vulnerable to hollow religion. Rather than investing in internal realities, such as our hunger for more of the Father's love and our passion for His presence, we put our trust in things that are seen.

This inevitably leads to other orphan characteristics, such as being jealous and competitive. We become envious when we see others with more spectacular buildings, services, and numbers and we whip our congregations into giving more so that we can build bigger. When we do this we are no longer trusting in our Father to provide but rather relying on the finances generated by our performance. This is hollow religion. It does not satisfy the soul's deepest desire which is for intimacy with the God who lavishly provides for us as His sons and daughters.

Jesus taught us to approach our Father and ask for Him to provide our daily bread. Through Jesus we are offered a relationship in which our generous Father promises to provide what we need when we need it. The manna in the wilderness is an example of this. God gave the people of Israel what they needed each day, for that day. The same is true for us. Our Father provides for us every day. This encourages us to live in a constant trusting relationship with Him. We are no longer orphans, operating from the poverty mindset that wants to grab everything we can and hope that others don't receive anything. Instead we rejoice that we have a generous Dad and cheer when others experience His extravagance. That way we are able to focus on developing the family business rather than being preoccupied with storing up riches for ourselves and becoming bitter when others succeed.

## The Protective Father

In the final part of the Lord's Prayer, Jesus taught us to ask for forgiveness, to release forgiveness to others when they hurt us and to pray for protection from the evil one.

A good father protects his children. There are few instincts in the world more powerful than that of a parent wanting to protect their children. Ask any parent whose child is being bullied at school or who runs out towards a road. God is the best Father in the universe and He promises to protect us.

One Sunday morning I was praying at the beginning of the day for our services during the day ahead. As I prayed I had a very strange spiritual experience which I can only describe as feeling like I was in a different realm. If you have seen the Lord of the Rings movies, this was similar to when Frodo places the ring on his finger and sees colours and movement belonging to another dimension altogether. In the midst of this experience I sensed a small child running behind me and rushing out into a road. A fast moving car was driving towards him. In the vision I stood out in the road, held my hand up and shouted, "No!" I felt as if the boy was one of my sons. After the experience I was shaking and praying for God's protection over my family.

After church that day my wife was talking to some close friends. Just before the service their son, aged two, had followed his dad out onto the street as he packed the car. He had wandered out into the road. A car was driving at speed down their street and the dad only became aware at the last minute that his son was in danger. The boy was fine; he had pulled back just in time behind their car, narrowly avoiding a horrific accident.

God wants to protect us and our children and He empowers us to pray for that protection for ourselves and others at critical moments. I can't claim that my prayers saved that boy's life that day but I'm really glad I was spiritually alert and listening to the Holy Spirit.

We need to live in close relationship with our Father and be alert to His promptings for protection. We are not to live in fear, as those who follow hollow religion do, safeguarding every possession. We are to live in faith. As Paul says in Ephesians 6, our battle is not against flesh and blood. In the same letter he mentions "the heavenly realms" five times. This unseen realm is where the battle rages. We are not to live in fear because our Father is stronger than the enemy. We are to trust in His revelation and resources.

Orphans cannot live this way. Instead of living from a centre of love and trust they live from a centre of fear and suspicion. Hollow religion is the inevitable consequence. The orphan's response to the unseen enemy is to protect everything, to bunker down in fear. Orphans accordingly become increasingly static, sticking to the safety of the familiar, denying themselves the possibility of pioneering beyond their comfort zones into new territories and opportunities.

The joy of living as sons and daughters is that we bask under the protection and direction of our Father. This means that we can take risks and live dynamic lives, trusting Him to protect us, to warn us of danger and defend us when we get it wrong.

This also means that we are not vulnerable to the taunts of the accuser. Satan's nature is to constantly bombard us with accusations, to pull us down with shame, condemnation and self-hatred, all of which hinder us from building God's kingdom. God our Father protects us from the voice of the accuser through speaking words of forgiveness, acceptance and affirmation. This is not possible in hollow religion where orphans bow to the condemning voice of the father of lies rather than the loving voice of the Father of lights.

## The Wonderful Cross

Jesus taught us to pray to our Heavenly Father for His presence, provision and protection. To pray in such an intimate way is radically different from hollow religion. Instead of working to earn these things, we reach out our hands like little children and simply receive them as our inheritance.

Fallen man, separated from God, has always sought to earn God's favour, whatever the era and whatever the culture. This has resulted in countless rituals, sacrifices, incantations, patterns of prayer, and so on. It has produced complicated and irrational laws and commandments.

Fallen humanity feels acutely its separation from God and tries to bridge the gap using human resources and effort, seeking to earn the presence, provision and protection of God through religious performance.

The extraordinary truth of the Gospel is that God has already done what such religious striving attempts to do. Our loving Father has built the bridge from His side, sending His one and only Son to bring His unmerited favour to earth and release an extravagant inheritance to those who believe in His Son and receive the gift of His Holy Spirit.

This is so different from hollow religion! Religion, from earliest times, has always sought to bridge this gap from earth to heaven. In all of these endeavours, offering sacrifices has been central. In her book Sacrifice and the Death of Christ, biblical scholar and historian Frances Young classifies three main types of sacrifice in the ancient world: gift-sacrifices, communion sacrifices and sin-offerings.[iii] The underlying motive behind all of these was to gain the favour of the gods in order to receive their blessings.

In the early Hebrew culture, Yahweh commanded a similar system of sacrifices to be offered by His people only with one significant difference – they were to be offered within the context of a loving covenant relationship. Another difference was that human sacrifice was absolutely unthinkable.

Having entered the Promised Land and later established the monarchy, the people of Israel made the Temple in Jerusalem the focal point for this system of sacrifices. When the Babylonians invaded Jerusalem and took the people of Judah into exile, they destroyed the Temple and thus the sacrificial system. In exile, the Jewish people faced a crisis as they could no longer reach up to heaven, appealing to God's forgiveness and favour through the offering of sacrifices on the brazen altar in the outer court of the Temple. How were they to worship God?

Through this time the prophets speak a repeated message against offering sacrifices. God had revealed to them that the sacrifices of the people of Judah had become religious and were no longer an act of authentic, heart-felt worship. The clearest summary of this prophetic message is found in Hosea 6.6: "For I desire steadfast love and not sacrifice, the knowledge of God rather than burnt offerings." Yahweh was no longer satisfied with a sacrificial system based on hollow religion. These offerings were no longer the expression of a covenant relationship with Him. They were the outworking of meaningless traditions that had risen from a belief that God's favour had to be earned.

Moving into the New Testament era, God chose to fulfil and indeed replace the sacrifices of the Temple by sending His only son to be the once-and-for-all sacrifice for sin. The death of Jesus is the final act of propitiation designed to bridge the gap between God and us. This saving death did away with all further need for religious sacrifices and attempts to earn His favour. The Father's favour is permanently and unconditionally offered, removing any religious burdens from us.

We are now the beloved children of a generous Father. Looking up to Him, honouring Him, spending time in His presence and trusting Him is how He has designed us to live. As we dismantle the lies that separate us from Him, we move from attempting to gain his favour through hollow religion to enjoying His favour poured out through His kindness.

Hollow religion views God as distant and demanding and so creates forms of worship and ways of living that are an attempt to get from Him what we want. But God has revealed himself as a loving Father. He has invited us into an intimate relationship, given us an inheritance and promised to protect us.

Believing that will lead us out of hollow religion.

## Notes

i. Shared with permission from a personal email. Baxter shares more of this in his upcoming book Patmos.

ii. From an article published on 12/8/11 www.chiefrabbi.org

iii. Frances Young Sacrifice and the Death of Christ p21.

# 6

# The Unreligious Son

The Apostle Paul encourages us to set our sights on the realities of heaven where Jesus is enthroned in glory (Colossians 3:1 NLT).

Anyone who wants to be free from hollow religion must not only learn to look up into the adoring eyes of Abba Father. They must also learn to fix their gaze on the exalted Jesus.

Jesus is the antidote to futile religion. All religion is ultimately hollow because it represents the human attempt to bridge the great divide between earth and heaven. Only when a person comes to understand that Jesus alone is the Mediator does religion end and relationship begin. Jesus is the only way to the Father. There is no other route by which we can arrive at an intimate communion with God.

The second part of looking up therefore consists of lifting our heads, hearts and hands to Jesus. Those who enter into an everlasting friendship with the living Lord Jesus embark on an adventure that is completely free from hollow religion. It is relationship. It is reality. It is everything that religion cannot give us.

In this and the following chapters we are going to look at why this is. Why is it that following Jesus frees us from the bondage of religion? What is it specifically about the nature of Jesus of Nazareth that is so different from religion? How does an authentic relationship with Him make a man or a woman allergic to hollow religion?

In this chapter we will see that Jesus is the Father's radical solution to religion. If religion symbolises man's attempt to reach up to where God is, Jesus represents God's achievement in coming down to where man is. Jesus, being fully God and fully man, alone brings man back to God.

## See Jesus, See the Father

"In these last days he has spoken to us by his Son, whom he appointed the heir of all things, through whom also he created the world. He is the radiance of the glory of God and the exact imprint of his nature, and he upholds the universe by the word of his power." (Hebrews 1:2–3)

"He is the image of the invisible God." (Colossians 1:15)

In these two passages the same claim is made: that Jesus is the complete revelation of what God is truly like. He is God's full self-disclosure – the master key, the template, the plumbline, the ace of trumps. If we want to know what God is really like, we have to begin with Jesus and work outwards from there. Anything that is claimed about God but which is inconsistent with what we see in Jesus should not be given the same level of authority. Jesus Christ is the centre of all that we can say about what God is really like.

Greg Boyd puts it like this: "This centre is Jesus Christ, the one who perfectly reveals to us the love God eternally is, who perfectly embodies the love God has for us, who perfectly models the love we're to have toward others, and who is the means by which we enter into a loving covenantal, faith-based relationship with God."[i]

This is a big truth and its implications are huge. In recent years I have applied this test to everything I believe about God: "Is it consistent with the revelation of God's character found in Jesus?" When I have discovered areas of my understanding of God that are inconsistent with this truth, I have realigned them. I have immersed myself in reading the Gospels to make sure that everything I believe about God is visible in the life, ministry, death and resurrection of Jesus Christ. As Jesus said, "He who has seen me has seen the Father" (John 14:9).

A lot of hollow religious thinking is based on a view of God that is not primarily derived from the revelation God has given us of Himself in Jesus. In many ways the Church has historically been guilty of this when it has based its understanding of God on Western (and particularly Greek) philosophy. Or it has based its view on the partial revelation of God in the Old Testament.

This is exactly what Jesus' contemporaries did. The Pharisees and the Sadducees had a partial revelation of God based on the Old Testament. They were so fixated with it that they were unwilling to recognise the complete revelation provided by Jesus. When a person bases their theology on Greek philosophy or the Old Testament (or some mix of the two), it results in a view of God as distant and disinterested. This is not a perspective rooted in Jesus and consequently enforces the distance lie upon which hollow religion is built.

More from Greg Boyd: "Jesus came into this world and died on the cross to blow apart all deceptive mental pictures of God that we've been enslaved to since the original fall and that lie at the root of all idolatry and sin ... The revelation of God's true character on Calvary was the explosion of light that in principle expelled all darkness and the explosion of love that in principle destroyed all hate. It was the revelation that in principle defeated Satan and the fallen powers and thereby freed humans to be reconciled to God (Colossians 2:14-15; cf. Hebrews 2:14; 1 John 3:8)."[ii]

Anyone who wants to walk away from hollow religion must therefore establish a Jesus-centred approach to all theology - to all understanding and speaking about God.

This is exactly what I have tried to do in my own life.

Jesus is therefore the alternative to religion. As we look at the life, death and resurrection of Jesus, we can see fairly quickly that He is the antithesis of what I have defined as hollow religion. He embodies the exact opposite of the five characteristics of hollow religion (chapter 1).

Jesus demonstrated the power of God rather than an empty form of godliness. He came not to judge the world but to save it. He taught not from an accumulation of knowledge (although clearly He knew the Scriptures well) but from a living relationship with the Father. He was profoundly dynamic and challenged empty tradition, bringing radical change everywhere He went. And He lived as Son of God, confident of His Father's love and inheritance, never once attempting to earn His Father's favour.

## Radical Jesus

Jesus confronted hollow religion even before He was born because in heaven a decision was made that He would be conceived in the womb of a virgin and born nine months later. That was scandalous to the religious mindset. The idea that the most Holy God of the universe should be born to a young Israeli woman was outrageous. Even today the religious mind finds it difficult to comprehend that the infinite became an infant in Jesus. The religious mind can only conceive of reaching up to where God is in all His distant majesty. But in Jesus we see the opposite trajectory. We see divine love coming down to our level, to be made incarnate in the dust and dirt of an animal's shelter.

In recent years I've approached the Christmas season by asking my church leadership team, "What does an unreligious Christmas look like?" We attempt to listen to God for His vision, recognising that Christmas celebrations can very easily become about form rather than power, about static tradition rather than dynamic encounter.

The story of Jesus' birth in the Gospels is the opposite of hollow religion. There are angelic visitations, prophetic dreams and extraordinary miracles everywhere. Jesus' life as a man was profoundly unreligious too. He modelled bold resistance to religious convention right from the start of His ministry by turning water into wine at a party and declaring that He was the fulfilment of Isaiah 61 in his own synagogue.

Jesus consistently confronted Pharisees, Sadducees, Scribes and anyone else who exhibited self-righteous tendencies. He broke the Law by fellowshipping with sinners, healing the sick on the Sabbath and claiming that He was God. Reading the Gospels is therefore a profoundly unsettling experience for the religious person. Jesus so clearly refuses to be boxed in by religious traditions.

Sometimes I find Jesus' radicalism unsettling as well. When I allow my theology to become too settled, and use it as the basis for criticising others, I find that Jesus challenges me afresh in the Gospels and stirs me to think and act differently. He is compassionate and tender to the sick and troubled but blunt and direct to those who think they have it altogether.

## An Unreligious Life

Those who have chosen the way of hollow religion have always sought to exert control over Kingdom people throughout church history. One aspect of Jesus that inspires me is His total resistance to being controlled by other people, especially religious people. In Luke 4, having shocked everyone in the synagogue by declaring that he was the fulfilment of Isaiah 61, we first of all read that "all spoke well of him and marvelled at the gracious words that were coming from his mouth." But then Jesus publicly rebukes the whole town for their unbelief and they attempt to throw Him off a cliff. The Gospel account says that He passes through them. He simply walks away.

On another occasion in Luke 12 someone calls out from the crowd, asking Jesus to step into a dispute which the man is having with his brother. Jesus refuses to put himself in the position of judge and goes on to tell a parable challenging greed.

See how different Jesus is! When there's a storm, He sleeps. When others are sailing, He walks on water. When a scribe offers to follow Him he replies, "Foxes have holes and birds of the air have nests, but the Son of Man has nowhere to lay his head."

As Jesus enters Jerusalem on the Sunday before Passover the crowds greet Him, expecting him to seize power by leading a revolution against the Roman occupying powers. Instead, He goes to the Temple and clears out the moneychangers and pigeon-sellers.

When Jesus is arrested by force in the garden of Gethsemane, it becomes clear that it's by His choice that this happens. He is allowing events to unfold the way that they do. His enemies are therefore not in control, even though they think they are. Jesus is calling the shots!

At His trial, Jesus continues to be in control. He either reflects back questions or remains silent. He doesn't bend under the control of others but lives in total obedience to His Father in heaven and Him alone.

Jesus is utterly dynamic, embodies genuine freedom and throws off all attempts to restrict or control Him.

## Honouring Women

Jesus confronts religious conventions and traditions that grew up over time and which contradicted the ethos of the culture of heaven.

This is especially true in His attitude towards women. The culture in which He was born was profoundly patriarchal and male-dominated. Women were not honoured. Their testimony in a court of law was deemed worthless. They were very much second-class citizens. Men held power in the home and the city. Women were not empowered to lead. They certainly weren't regarded as having equal status with men.

Then Jesus enters the stage of history, sounding a different note, embodying a different ethos. In a culture in which men weren't allowed to speak to women, Jesus has friends who are women. He teaches and empowers women. He even allows women whom His contemporaries regarded as shameful to wash His feet. The coming of Jesus and then subsequently the outpouring of the Holy Spirit brings a dramatic counter-cultural revolution. Women are now honoured. So are children. So are the poor. So are all those whom religion oppressed.

One of the foul fruits of hollow religion has been gender inequality in the church. This has more to do with the culture of the world (or in the case of 21st century Britain, the culture of previous generations). Hollow religion clings to human forms of power rather than yielding to God and trusting the power of the Holy Spirit to bring life. Often this results in power being held by one gender over another, which can be hugely destructive.

One evening at our church, as we prayed into becoming an

"unreligious church," an older lady said to me, "I feel like I've been in a straightjacket all my Christian life [over thirty years]. I thought it was normal. Now for the first time I'm tasting a new freedom. It's wonderful!"

Those are some of the most encouraging words I've ever heard! Later I discovered that a large part of the straightjacket was her Church background. Women were restricted from playing any role in the prayer, worship or teaching life of the Church. Women were second-class citizens.

How different from Jesus!

Jesus brought freedom to women from the control exerted over them by men. He liberated women from those who clung to hollow religion as an excuse for using power to keep them from enjoying what they did. Jesus truly honoured women.

## The Revolutionary Teacher

Then there is His teaching. What Jesus teaches is also completely unreligious and in many cases directly confronts hollow religious mindsets.

One example of this is his use of parables. Jesus tells simple, invitational stories which are pregnant with profound kingdom truths. Those who listen don't need knowledge or education to understand Him. Instead He makes the Kingdom of God accessible to all by telling open-ended stories that invite us to ponder and meditate further, that for two thousand years have stimulated people from all cultures and educational backgrounds to seek more understanding of the culture of heaven.

Not surprisingly it is often the religious who don't understand Jesus! One example is found in Mark 12:28-33:

"And one of the scribes came up and heard them disputing with one another, and seeing that he answered them well, asked him, 'Which commandment is the most important of all?' Jesus answered, 'The most important is, "Hear, O Israel: The Lord our God, the Lord is one. And you shall love the Lord your God with all your heart and with all your soul and with all your mind and with all your strength." The second is this: "You shall love your neighbour as yourself." There is no other commandment greater than these.' And the scribe said to him, 'You are right, Teacher. You have truly said that he is one, and there is no other besides him. And to love him with all the heart and with all the understanding and with all the strength and to love one's neighbour as oneself."'

Can you see how the scribe in this story misunderstands Jesus? Can you spot how he makes a critical error? Set on one side what Jesus says and on the other what the scribe says as he quotes Jesus words back to Him. Can you see the subtle difference?

Here's the point: Jesus' quotation contains the words heart, soul, mind and strength.

The scribe quotes these words back, using the words heart, understanding and strength.

The scribe completely misses out the word "soul".

Why is this so important? The soul is the seat of our emotions, passions, affections and desires. Unlike our physical bodies, it is invisible and intangible.

The scribe has missed the point: Jesus came to reconnect us to our loving Father. He came to reunite our hearts to the Father heart of God. He came to lead us into an affectionate relationship not an academic religion.

That involves the soul, our passion, not just our intellects!

The scribe makes a further mistake. He uses a completely different word from Jesus to describe our mind/intellect. In the original Greek language of the New Testament, Jesus uses the word dionoia, translated "mind". The scribe uses the word sunesis translated "understanding".

The word Jesus uses is full of dynamic motion; it literally means the movements and motions of our mind. The word the scribe uses describes something static; it means the established knowledge we have attained through study and learning.

God wants us to love Him with the motions of our minds: to love Him with our thinking; our pondering; our meditations on His character and kingdom. We don't need extensive knowledge for this and those who haven't benefitted from a formal education can still love Him in this way. This means that those with learning difficulties or neurological damage to their brains are able to love Him with their minds. Jesus is primarily looking for those whose minds are open to change not those whose minds are full of academic learning.

Jesus' teaching is not designed exclusively for those who have knowledge. He doesn't set tests nor does He put limitations on who can think about the Kingdom. Most importantly of all, He never withholds knowledge in order to exercise power over others, which is the way of hollow religion. Instead He gives Kingdom truths open access; they are freely given to all those humble enough to receive. As we read in Matthew 11:25: "At that time Jesus declared, 'I thank you, Father, Lord of heaven and earth, that you have hidden these things from the wise and understanding and revealed them to little children.'"

One of the joys of parenting is helping children to engage in God's truths. Anyone involved in children's ministry or in parenting will have stories of the amazing ways children pick up truth and are able to understand God's Kingdom - not in perfect neat, systematic theological reflections, but in honest questioning and trustful pondering.

Children often understand Jesus better than adults.

The childlike understand Him better than the sophisticated.

## Embrace Not Exclusion

Jesus is clear that our role is not to judge, nor to condemn others. In Matthew 7:7 He insists, "Judge not, that you be not judged." He goes further to say that the focus of His ministry is not judgement but salvation: "For God did not send His son into the world to condemn the world, but in order that the world might be saved through him" (John 3.17).

A major characteristic of hollow religion is judgmentalism and condemnation, resulting in rejection, exclusion and criticism. The knock-on effects of this are division and factions, defensiveness and a fear of punishment.

Judgement creates a culture of pulling down, not building up. That is the culture of the Pharisees, not Jesus.

One result of judgement is exclusion. Those with power become judges of who is "in" and who is "out". This is a common characteristic of religion: the creation of a "club of the acceptable" and an exclusion zone for those who are deemed unacceptable.

Initially this exclusion is often justified on the grounds of protecting the doctrinal or ethical purity of the group and the pursuit of a (religious) form of holiness. However, sooner or later prejudice, self-protection and superiority inevitably infiltrate this and the outcome is humanly drawn lines around the Kingdom and insurmountable barriers designed to keep out those who are weak and hurting.

One of the most challenging issues facing the Church today is the dramatic way in which cultural change in the West has led to very different perspectives on sexuality, gender roles and understanding of authority. Our modern mass media has changed the way these things are debated and understood. Often discussions about these topics are highly charged emotionally. They are fuelled by past pain and experiences of rejection.

A few years ago at a social occasion I met a prominent clergyman who regularly writes in national newspapers and other media and is often critical of those parts of the Church different from his own. I asked him why he spoke out in this way. He shared honestly and vulnerably about the pain he experienced at university from other Christians judging and rejecting him due to his Church background.

So often the Church excludes people and in the process reinforces the rejection that they already feel.

In the process, hollow religion triumphs.

Instead of experiencing embrace, people experience exclusion. This is the furthest remove from the way of Jesus.

One of the fruits of judgmentalism is criticism. This can also derive from a desire to protect the moral or doctrinal purity of a religious group. In my experience, criticising others is rife within the Church.

There is a place for being gatekeepers – for leaders guarding what comes in and goes out of the church family. If you read the Pastoral Epistles in the New Testament (1 and 2 Timothy, Titus, etc) you will see that a significant portion of these letters is devoted to urging the people of God to be on guard against those who would infiltrate the fold and distort the message of the Gospel. Those called to be shepherds in the Church are tasked to keep wolves from the doors.

However, it needs to be remembered that these passages apply to people who perpetrate significant deviations from the primary truths of the Bible, not to people whose beliefs, backgrounds and lifestyles differ from our own. Hollow religion develops a culture where criticism is justified, sometimes even encouraged, with very harmful results.

This criticism is dangerous because it tends to focus on what is seen. Judgements are made on the basis of external appearances or second-hand gossip. This leads to a prejudicial preoccupation with external behaviour rather than on internal factors such as relationship with God and personal integrity. The visible sins of others are judged harshly, whilst the more insidious internal sins of pride, stubborn rebellion, unbelief, self-hatred and many others are left to fester and grow unchallenged. The result is that people become what Jesus called "whitewashed tombs" - clean on the outside but dead on the inside.

A further by-product of this is defensiveness, which is rooted in the fear of punishment or rejection. Where criticism is normal and justified, people get hurt and where people get hurt they become afraid and defend themselves.

There are some friendships where I feel unsafe, maybe because there has been a track-record of mockery or because they are relationships in which my perspectives have been aggressively challenged. In some of them there has been such a high level of inconsistency that I've had no idea what reaction I'll receive. Intuitively in such contexts I think before I speak. I don't disclose certain parts of myself, whether thoughts or past actions. I avoid vulnerability and become ponderous, withdrawn and restricted. Or I become verbose and over-explain things in order to defend myself.

Relationships like these are draining; we use up energy to defend ourselves rather than become energised through open, honest, intimate friendship.

In contrast, there are friendships where I know I am safe; I can speak honestly. I have space to express myself. I am free to be me. In these friendships there's invariably a culture of love and honour and a lack of judgementalism. This just goes to highlight the fact that we flourish when we know we are accepted.

In the parable of the talents in Matthew 25, the third servant is afraid of the anticipated reaction from his master so he hides his talent and the investment doesn't grow.

A few years ago my mentor lovingly pointed out that my preaching was defensive. Whenever I preached, it was as if I had an invisible critic sitting on my shoulder who was concerned about theological questions the congregation weren't asking. I immediately recognised this as true. My constant thoughts in preparation and preaching were, "Is this watertight?" "Could I back that up in a theology essay?" "Is that sound doctrinally?" I was using up a lot of time and energy protecting my sermons from the anticipated criticism and nit-picking of imaginary judges. I was not free to share God's Word to equip, encourage and challenge His children.

## A Bland Grey Landscape

The real danger here is that hollow religion makes us dull. It's in the enemy's best interest for Christians to become boring. When we use most of our mental energy to defend ourselves, when we substitute fun for a fear of being mocked, when we use the opportunities we have to speak merely to justify ourselves or earn approval, we become boring.

As a youth worker I was invited to speak at a family member's church. The congregation was considerably older and more formal than me and as I shook hands with them at the door they thanked me for being "refreshing."

I went back a few years later, whilst I was training for ordination. I had done more study of the Bible using commentaries by then.

I had studied the theological debates surrounding the subject of my sermon. This time I had carefully crafted each word, phrase and sentence. Once again members of the congregation thanked me and smiled on the way out.

Years later, my uncle told me that a number of the older ladies had asked in the following weeks: "What happened to him? He used to have such raw passion and fire in his belly. How did he lose it? He's become grey and dull."

Jesus loved to teach people, to feed them God's truth, to reveal the Kingdom of God to them, to instruct them in Kingdom living and challenge sinful thinking. He wasn't concerned about the jibes and snipes from the Scribes and Pharisees. He had a range of responses to them: tricking them; ignoring them; provoking them or, as we saw earlier, publicly rebuking them. Jesus refused to allow the restrictive culture of criticism to hinder Him in any way because He knew He wasn't under their judgement. He was under the Father's unconditional approval. Jesus was therefore never boring. He was free to be radical and revelatory. He spoke as a much loved son not a religious orphan.

Another tragic result of defensiveness is that it hinders us from being vulnerable. When we are afraid of being judged, we hide our weaknesses, mistakes and sin and the roots of hurts and false beliefs about God which cause them. When these roots of pain and craving for comfort are hidden, we deny God access to them and so we are unable to receive His healing love and power to set us free. This in turn means that we have nothing to offer others except a superficial faith based on appearances.

In a hollow religious culture of criticism, the fear of rejection is used as a powerful means of control. There are unwritten implications and sometimes anecdotal precedents for what will happen to someone who does not tow a party line or who chooses to be vulnerable. In such a context people can minister in a subconscious attempt to gain acceptance and favour from those they respect. This restricts adventure, risk and creativity. The results are legalism and fear.

When this happens, a bland greyness pervades everything.

A Kingdom culture, where people are trusted as children of God, filled with the Spirit and anointed to bring revelation, is completely different. Creativity thrives, adventures are pursued, fresh initiatives are welcomed and peoples' gifts and destinies are discovered and released.

A few years ago the Lord spoke a very simple, very clear word to me: "More mess, less control." It's become a motto for my ministry and leadership style. When people start waking up to the truth that they're not going to be criticised, they find a new freedom which allows them to grow to maturity.

The role of leaders is to develop a Kingdom culture where this freedom can thrive. In such a culture there is a strong attitude of trust and the security to receive not only encouragement and coaching but also constructive reflection (rather than harsh criticism) where that is necessary.

We are to offer forgiveness, support and restoration when mistakes are made, rather than rejection and exclusion. We are also to exercise wisdom and discernment and release the right people into leadership and ministry at the right time. Within a Kingdom culture we set people up to thrive, to display their supernatural talents.

Those who are secure in the Father's love do not spend time either being defensive or defending themselves. Defending ourselves is in any event a sin and inconsistent with true Kingdom life - with what Jesus modelled. As we see in 1 Peter 2:21-23:

"Christ also suffered for you, leaving you an example, so that you might follow in his steps... When he was reviled, he did not revile in return; when he suffered he did not threaten, but continued entrusting himself to him who judges justly."

As we begin to recognise the restrictiveness of a defensive culture, we challenge that by following Jesus' example and choosing not to defend ourselves. When we are criticised and judged, we don't react by fighting back or by defending ourselves. We entrust ourselves to the One who is authorised to judge and allow our loving Father to be our protector, rather than take on the puffed up role of protecting His church and indulging in sibling rivalry.

Throughout Jesus' life, he taught and modelled how to live free from religion. He lived in full submission to God without legalism and without being bound to the traditions of His culture. His teaching introduced a vision and understanding that expressed the character of His Father. He demonstrated the power of God rather than merely a form of godliness and He directly confronted the established systems of religion which He saw controlling and restricting people from the life that He came to bring them.

In this respect, Jesus introduced a lifestyle that was totally at odds with that encapsulated by many of the Pharisees He encountered. Many of these Pharisees, who saw themselves as the true defenders of the Jewish faith, were the very epitome of hollow religion. When they encountered Jesus, hollow religion came face-to-face with heavenly reality.

As we will see in the next chapter, something had to give.

## Notes

i. Greg Boyd Benefit of the doubt p170.

ii. ibid. pg.188.

# 7

# The Woeful Pharisees

Jesus was blunt and confrontational at times, particularly when he faced the Pharisees, Sadducees and Teachers of the Law. When we read in the Gospels about Jesus' encounters with them we realise that He really didn't like their hollow religion with all its hypocrisy.

"Hypocrite" was originally a Greek term used for an actor who wore a mask on stage. Jesus used this word to sum up the Pharisees, highlighting the inconsistency between their external appearance and their hearts. The Pharisees had the form of religion but without the power of the Holy Spirit.

When the Lord first started waking me up to the reality of hollow religion I asked him the dangerous question: "Lord, would you put a plumbline into my life and expose some of my hollow religion?" He led me to work through the Seven Woes in Matthew 23 as a checklist of hollow religion. It was clear from God's presence with me that day that His intentions weren't for me to study Scripture just to build up my knowledge and then teach others! He took my prayer seriously (I'm sure He was waiting for it) and took the opportunity for His word to work as a scalpel, cutting through my life and revealing the extent that I was living according to hollow religion, not His kingdom. It was a painful and deeply challenging experience but I look back on it with joy when I consider the change that's happened since.

Like the serpent who invented it, the demonic scheme of hollow religion is slippery and subtle. It masquerades as normal Christianity. Today many of us have become so accustomed to it that we believe it is authentic.

In Matthew 15:13 Jesus links the Pharisees with the parable of the weeds in Matthew 13. In that parable it is initially difficult to distinguish between the healthy life-giving wheat and the life-stealing weeds.

See how vital it is for us to learn to distinguish between hollow religion and authentic Christianity. That way we can renounce the lies of the enemy, repent of choosing hollow religion, and learn to become a Kingdom people.

If you're willing for Him to shine His light on the hollow religion in your life, then read on. Take time after each point in the next section and ask the Holy Spirit to convict you where you've embraced hollow religion in your life.

## Introducing Matthew 23

Verses 1-3: "Then Jesus said to the crowds and to his disciples, 'The scribes and the Pharisees sit on Moses' seat, so do and observe whatever they tell you, but not the works they do. For they preach, but do not practise.'"

Jesus begins with an extraordinarily challenging perspective on authority. "They sit on Moses seat, so do what they say." Even though he is about to lay into their hypocrisy, Jesus still tells the crowd to recognise and submit to the authority of the office they hold. That, in itself, is a significant challenge to our modern

Western approach to authority.

"They preach, but they do not practise..." I thought I'd always sought to live in line with my own preaching and only to preach what I'm willing to live myself. The Lord showed me that day a number of ways where that hadn't been the case with my teaching around that time. I was cut to the heart when I considered the contrast between what I was publicly portraying of myself (the form) and the internal reality of how, in so many ways, I wasn't living what I believed.

Verses 5-7: "They do all their deeds to be seen by others. For they make their phylacteries broad and their fringes long, and they love the place of honour at feasts and the best seats in the synagogues and greetings in the marketplaces and being called rabbi by others."

Reputation can become an idol in the Church. We know that to pursue it is wrong and to be motivated by growing or maintaining it is sinful. But when I came to this afresh, with the loving conviction of the Holy Spirit, this verse painted clearly for me the subtle ways in which I had slipped into the same patterns as the Pharisees. I don't wear Phylacteries or any special robes to pray but when a visitor sat in my usual seat on the front row at church, I caught myself being offended. There are subtle ways in every denomination in which those of us called to lead can begin to enjoy reputation, title and status in an unhealthy manner. When we do, we forget that its origin is hollow religion and the desire for power and control that goes with it.

Verses 11-12: "The greatest among you shall be your servant. Whoever exalts himself will be humbled, and whoever humbles himself will be exalted."

Servant leadership is profoundly unreligious; it's the very opposite of what we have seen as the roots of hollow religion:

the human desire for power and control. The raw biblical truth we see here is that God's children, secure in who they already are, are to humble themselves at every level. The fallen human nature seeks to exalt itself and under the façade of hollow religion gives reasons why we should promote ourselves, push ourselves forwards, and why we're entitled to pursue places of influence and opportunity.

But God our Father is an empowering Father. He passionately believes in you and me and He really wants to see us thrive. He has placed extraordinary gifts and dreams and anointing within you, as a gift to the church and the world. He is thoroughly committed to empowering and releasing you into opportunities to be a blessing to others whom He also loves. Hollow religion occurs when we try and take control of that process for Him, out of fear that He might abandon us and leave us and demote us.

* * *

In that initial prophetic prayer time when I discerned hollow religion in my life, the lie accompanying it was that God would abandon me in ministry if I didn't get everything right. I was worn out and burned out on the inside because I was driven by a fear that if I didn't work hard, make the right connections, build up a good reputation, I'd find myself attempting to lead a dead church, unable to bring reform even to the brass polishing rotas! God showed me that He had called me to ministry for a purpose. He reminded me that He had designed my life to be fruitful. A future of frustration over pointless religious battles wasn't what He had lined up for me. That was a wonderful release.

## The Seven Woes

That was just the introduction to Matthew 23! Now we move onto what's known as the Seven Woes.

### 1st Woe, Verse 13

"Woe to you, scribes and Pharisees, hypocrites! For you shut the kingdom of heaven in people's faces. For you neither enter yourselves nor allow those who would enter to go in."

One of the most intriguing and impacting things I have read in recent years is the first chapter of Rob Bell's book Velvet Elvis, particularly the part where he defines the modern evangelical obsession with assessing "who is in and who is out." It's such a simple way of describing hollow religion, which involves judging those who are saved and who are not. Hollow religion sets up exclusion zones. It turns the Kingdom into a closed rather than an open family.

Part of our desire for power and control is manifested in creating safe clubs, built on agreement with some and disagreement with others, and using that as an excuse to reject those with whom we disagree.

One of my father's favourite phrases, spoken ironically, was, "Let's create a club so we can keep other people out." Timothy Keller writes: "We must not depict the gospel as primarily joining something (Christ's kingdom program) but as receiving something (Christ's finished work)."[i]

The Pharisees clearly had an exclusivist philosophy. They were only willing to accept those who performed to certain standards, rigidly agreed with certain doctrines and ultimately came under their control. Jesus certainly wasn't willing to do so and hence they very quickly came into confrontation with him.

We will look at the wider aspects of judgementalism later. The concern here is specifically the religious act of taking upon ourselves the role of judging who is in or out of the Kingdom. When we do this we miss God's heart of welcome, inclusion and grace.

In years gone by I have met a disproportionate number of

later middle-aged men who have rejected Jesus and constructed a damaging secular worldview. Many of them have shared how this dates back to their experience of being rejected by evangelical groups at university who were rigid about who was in and who was out and judgemental of anyone with an inquisitive mind. In each case hearing their stories of rejection by "the club" has sounded exactly like Jesus' description of the Pharisees shutting the Kingdom of Heaven in peoples' faces. My personal challenge is: "Where have I done the same thing myself?"

Notice also a second aspect to this Woe: "For you neither enter yourselves nor allow those who would enter to go in."

As children of God we are invited to enter the Kingdom of Heaven right now. We don't have to wait until we die. Over recent years I've seen the church believe, receive and engage with this in a new way.

In 2 Corinthians 12 Paul talks about a man he knows being caught up into the third heaven. In Ephesians 2:6 Paul describes us as "seated with Christ in heavenly places" in the present tense. Hebrews 4:16 encourages us to approach the throne of grace with confidence.

Jesus opened up the way for us to be reconciled with the Father who is in heaven. His criticism of the Pharisees was that they didn't enter the Kingdom of Heaven themselves. Hollow religion does that; it results in us claiming to live as citizens of heaven when in reality inhabiting a colony of slaves. The fact is we are invited to spend time in the throne room now. We are welcomed into the Kingdom now. Only hollow religion keeps us from accepting that invitation and sharing it with others. Here we are back once again to living at a distance from God. But God is an affectionate Father who invites us closer.

### 2nd Woe, Verse 15

"Woe to you, scribes and Pharisees, hypocrites! For you travel across sea and land to make a single proselyte, and when he becomes a proselyte, you make him twice as much a child of hell as yourselves."

Religion doesn't lack zeal. It goes to great lengths to get results. This can be the case in evangelism or other forms of convincing people to change. Yes we are encouraged to preach the Good News and persuade people to change. In growing the Kingdom we are to invite people into salvation and relationship with God. But that doesn't extend to exerting control over people and then making them into clones of ourselves!

We are each called to some form of leadership and our mandate is to release and empower God's children to become fully who they were made to be and to welcome greater creativity and diversity in the church family, even when that means rejoicing in people totally different from us.

Hollow religion, rooted in the desire to be in charge, reproduces itself and carries implicit pressure upon converts into behaving, speaking and thinking in ways which gain the approval of those who disciple them and usually those ways look a lot like themselves. The fear of rejection, allied to our natural desire for approval, can make us vulnerable to becoming clones, particularly of those we look up to.

If my goal as a hollow leader is to build and maintain the institution (because my reputation is tied to it), then I am very likely to exert power and control and create institutions of hollow religion rather than families of Kingdom power. In very real terms this is spiritual abuse. The trouble is it is usually disguised and camouflaged by an external form of good works. Deliberate spiritual abuse is a by-product of hollow religion and the misuse of authority.

As I recognised this, the Holy Spirit convicted me of the many ways in which I had used worldly methods of manipulating others (which were in fact religious control) to become just a little bit more like me.

### 3rd Woe, Verse 16:

"Woe to you, blind guides, who say, 'If anyone swears by the temple, it is nothing, but if anyone swears by the gold of the temple, he is bound by his oath.' You blind fools! For which is greater, the gold or the temple that has made the gold sacred?"

At this point Jesus enters into an argument with the scribes and Pharisees. This kind of heated discussion was typical of the rabbinical debates at the time, especially when it concerned issues to do with swearing oaths and the Temple.

Jesus points out that their thinking is too worldly. They have altogether missed the fact that the Temple was supposed to be the place where the glory of the presence of God dwelled.

Gold was a major feature of the Temple. The original design for the Tabernacle and Temple in Exodus 25-31 and 1 Kings 6-7 give details about a great deal of gold, especially in the Holy and Most Holy Places. Gold was symbolic of God's glory. However, Jesus argues that it was the Temple itself which was of real value not the gold used in its furnishings. While the gold pointed to God's glory, the Temple housed God's glory. Jesus therefore argues that it was the Temple which made the gold holy and not the other way around.

The natural man (i.e. the worldly person) is attracted to things of natural and worldly value such as gold. Hollow religion, which is natural and worldly, overemphasizes the value of such things, which is why Jesus criticizes the Scribes and the Pharisees.

Members of God's family have a different value system. We are attracted to the presence of God. Hollow religion focuses on man's gold. Authentic religion focuses on God's glory.

### 4th Woe, Verses 23-24:

"Woe to you, teachers of the law and Pharisees, you hypocrites! You give a tenth of your spices – mint, dill and cumin. But you have neglected the more important matters of the law – justice, mercy and faithfulness. You should have practised the latter, without neglecting the former. You blind guides! You strain out a gnat but swallow a camel."

It's irritating when a small bug lands in your drink on a summer's day but it's not quite the same as getting a spitting camel stuck in the back of your throat! Here Jesus uses comedy to emphasise the difference between petty religious laws and the Kingdom values of justice, mercy and faithfulness. The contrast between tithing herbs and obeying weightier matters of the Law shows us how ridiculous hollow religion is. Hollow religion clings to measurable details because they can become the external evidence to control and judge other people.

A passage like this can convict us in two ways. The first is when we have become so focussed on petty details that we miss the bigger picture. I've become aware of how often I retreat to focus on detailed accuracy for the sake of pride. God regularly calls us up to see the bigger story that He is writing about the life of His family. When we become lost in details they usually relate to the circumstances we are in right now and cause us to look down in despair. The bigger story is a story of hope and it raises our faith. The second is when my focus on details comes from a compulsion to be accurate as part of a pursuit of being right. The real reason I want to be right is my pride and the desire to promote myself, covering over the fear that I'll be rejected or mocked if I make a mistake. I don't believe Jesus is too worried about my being right in fussy details. He's concerned about me loving with the sacrificial agape love which He modelled for us.

### 5th Woe, Verses 25-26:

"Woe to you, teachers of the law and Pharisees, you hypocrites! You clean the outside of the cup and dish, but inside they are full of greed and self-indulgence. Blind Pharisee! First clean the inside of the cup and dish, and then the outside also will be clean." This is one of the most direct challenges to those who have form without power. We see this here with reference to cleanliness and holiness, which is at the root of salvation and the Gospel. The Law taught people how to clean the outside of their lives but God's desire is that this should be an expression of inner submission and generosity, two of the great hallmarks of love.

Jesus taught about the priority of our internal life above the external. "There is nothing outside a person that by going into him can defile him, but the things that come out of a person are what defile him." (Mark 7.15)

We have already seen that hollow religion gives attention to externals whereas God cares about our hearts. This applies to the whole area of holiness. God's desire is that we are holy because He is holy.

This holiness is not merely being clean on the outside (in our behaviour, which still matters to God) but in our hearts, where our motives are shaped. We live from our hearts out, not our actions in. There is a wonderful promise tucked at the end of this woe: when our hearts are cleansed, then our external lives will become clean too.

Whilst meditating on this woe, and the contrast between the

squeaky clean image I wanted to maintain and the greed and self-indulgence in my life, the Lord pointed to something in my own life through a linked passage of Scripture: "These people honour me with their lips, but their hearts are far from me" (Matthew 15.8, NIV). As this verse came to mind, I could saw a familiar scene in my imagination. I felt like I was worshipping in church - arms raised, eyes closed, voice in full flow, looking every bit the spiritual leader I wanted to portray. Behind this façade my mind was concentrating on something totally different - lunch, cricket, how the service was going and what notices I had to remember. I could feel the disconnection between the external appearance and my heart, which was far from God, giving Him no attention at all. The painful part was acknowledging that this was normal for me; the scene was typical. I was cut to the heart as I saw the reality of my own hollow religion.

### 6th Woe, Verses 27-28:

"Woe to you, scribes and Pharisees, hypocrites! For you are like whitewashed tombs, which outwardly appear beautiful, but within are full of dead people's bones and all uncleanness. So you also outwardly appear righteous to others, but within you are full of hypocrisy and lawlessness."

Jesus takes the same principle and 'ups the ante' considerably, just in case his listeners had missed the crucial importance of all this. It's one thing to talk about dirty and clean crockery and to emphasise the difference between externals and internals. But Jesus then goes on to teach that when religion becomes hollow it is a matter of life and death. In doing this he employs the striking analogy of whitewashed tombs.

The long-term results of hollow religion are death on the inside and perhaps, just as alarmingly to a Pharisee, "all kinds of uncleanness." The implication is that hollow religion reaps what it sows. It is built on the lie that we are separated from God and its eventual result is separation from God. If there is death at work on the inside, however nicely we cover it up and even bring that into church (like tombs), it is still death and the only solution to death is God's forgiveness and resurrection power in us. As long as I kept hiding the death within out of shame, God could not turn it around and bring me life.

### 7th Woe, Verses 29-32:

"Woe to you, scribes and Pharisees, hypocrites! For you build the tombs of the prophets and decorate the monuments of the righteous, saying, 'If we had lived in the days of our fathers, we would not have taken part with them in shedding the blood of the prophets.' Thus you witness against yourselves that you are sons of those who murdered the prophets. Fill up, then, the measure of your fathers."

This final woe requires explanation. Jesus is building on the illustration of the whitewashed tombs to expose the Pharisees' hypocrisy in two further ways. The first is in the way they compared themselves with their forefathers. By quoting their words about their forefathers, Jesus highlights their pride and self-righteousness. They are judging others from the past in order to promote themselves.

This is a trait I've noticed in myself and other church leaders. We criticise others from previous generations in order to promote our opinions and validate our teaching today. It's easy to knock the dead; they can't fight back in a debate. We often read their theology in books, forget how they lived it out, and then attack it in order to promote ourselves. It is both unjust and fruitless to judge others who lived without the benefits of the revelation that

God has given to us in our generation.

The second way in which Jesus exposes their hypocrisy is by showing that they are thinking merely in natural ways and missing spiritual truths. Whilst they are busy promoting themselves and displaying their self-righteousness, they miss the supernatural reality of generational sin and the spiritual inheritance from those they are judging. They set the previous generations up as opposite to them whilst in the spiritual realm they are closely linked to them.

Hollow religion functions only with natural thinking and misses out on spiritual realities and the ways of the Kingdom. In Colossians 2, before launching into a very significant passage on religion and judgementalism, Paul warns:

"See to it that no one takes you captive through hollow and deceptive philosophy, which depends on human tradition and the basic principles of this world rather than on Christ."

As we read this final woe, it reminds us to allow the Holy Spirit to convict us of our hollow religion rather than falling into the same religious trap as the Pharisees.

## Notes

i. Timothy Keller, Center Church, p30-31.

# 8

# Bridging the Gap

It cannot be denied that both those who are infected by hollow religion and those who are free from it respect and honour the cross of Christ. Both acknowledge that it is central to the Christian faith and in their different ways revere it. But there is a great difference between the hollow religious appreciation of the cross and the appreciation offered by someone who has been reconciled to the Father and who enjoys a living relationship with Him. What is this difference?

The short answer is that it is the difference between form and power. For the person steeped in hollow religion, the cross is merely a symbol. The reality to which that symbol points – transition from the life of sin to the life of a son – is missing from their lives. The symbol is all important. The reality to which that symbol points is secondary, veiled and obscured in the green mist of hollow religion. The cross therefore becomes more about decoration than transformation.

None of this is to say that symbolism is unimportant. Our hearts can process images more simply than words or ideas. God has spoken to millions of His children when they have meditated on the symbol of the cross. The problem with hollow religion, however, is that it makes a person deaf to the whispers of the Father. Built as it is on the lie about God's distance, hollow religion makes no room for the idea that the cross is the bridge on which human beings can return to the Father and enjoy profound relational intimacy and experiential closeness to Him.

Hollow religion cannot conceive of such joy.

Hollow religion turns the cross into a badge or identity marker for Christians. It downplays the transformation produced by the cross and instead uses the image of the cross as a banner under which religious tribes can rally.

As a banner the cross has been used this way for centuries. Nations and armies, claiming Christ as their own and displaying the cross upon their flags, have committed atrocities which are the very opposite of what Jesus modelled through his self-sacrificial death.

Furthermore, the cross has been abused as a relic too. Throughout Church history, alleged fragments of the wood to which Jesus was nailed have been said to contain supernatural powers. The problem with this is it has kept the focus on the cross as a relic rather than the cross as reconciliation.

Such superstitious uses of the symbol of the cross have even spread into non-Christian literature and film. In horror stories, crosses have often been deemed to have power to ward off vampires and "creatures of the night."

Fixation on the symbol or image of the cross is a sign of hollow religion. Whenever and wherever this happens, trivial issues become paramount – such as whether churches should display crucifixes with Jesus on them (emphasising his death) or not (emphasising his resurrection).

All this highlights the way in which religion focuses on form rather than power. Instead of stressing how the cross brings an end to the distance lie, religion has done the opposite.

## The Centrality of the Cross

What happened on the cross matters. Eternal destinies are determined as a result of the death of Jesus. In theological terms it is a primary issue.

The cross occupies a great deal of attention in the New Testament. Each of the Gospels contains lengthy descriptions of the last supper, betrayal, trial, torture and death of Jesus. The New Testament Book of Acts, as well as the Epistles, contains a great deal of writing about the cross.

In the New Testament the cross of Christ is described as a once-for-all event, with huge spiritual and natural consequences. The writers of the New Testament, inspired by the Holy Spirit, used a variety of images to describe and explain it. It is essential that we understand what Jesus achieved for us there.

Once again, these positive gifts from God have been twisted by hollow religion to produce debate and division. There are few subjects within the church which create more heated arguments, more criticism of others' perspectives, more labelling and factions, than the subject of the cross.

When the cross is approached religiously, focussing on its form rather than its power, the outcome can be ugly. But when we embrace the power of what Jesus did through His death, we find joyful freedom, including freedom from hollow religion.

What Jesus achieved on the cross is in fact the solution to hollow religion. His self-sacrificing, devil-defeating, sin-substituting, penalty-paying, choice to die in our place reconciles us to the Father.

It brings an end to the distance between man and God.

It brings lost children back to the Father's arms.

## The Cross as Reconciliation

The cross bridges the huge gap between earth and heaven.

On the cross Jesus reconciled God to humanity and humanity to God. The gulf between God and his creation, which gave space for hollow religion to grow, is mediated by Jesus death.

At the point of Jesus' death, the curtain in the Temple was ripped from top to bottom – an amazing picture of God tearing down the separation between Him and us.

In one of many Scriptures which describe our reconciliation to God, the Apostle Paul writes this:

"But now in Christ Jesus you who once were far off have been brought near by the blood of Christ." (Ephesians 2:13)

In the Hebrew Bible, the Jewish people understood what it was to be far from home. They had experienced this in both the Exodus and the Exile. Paul tapped into this bigger story when he wrote these words about the cross. Instead of being far away from the Promised Land (as in Jewish history before Christ), now Paul talks about how every human being has been far away from their heart's true home – the arms of the Father. That sense of distance has been solved at the cross. Our profound homesickness for God has been healed there.

The greatest loss caused to humanity in Eden was separation from God. Jesus' death was God's way of bringing His children back into relationship with Him. The cross is therefore essential for defeating hollow religion because what Jesus did for us at Calvary restores relationship with God. The initiative for this was from God's side (redemption) not ours (religion).

Timothy Keller defines religion as: "I obey; therefore I am accepted."[i] The cross demolishes that approach to God. You are accepted – welcomed, loved, valued, honoured, affirmed and precious – because Jesus died in your place. You don't ever need to live separately from God any more.

There is a great deal in the New Testament which teaches us about what God did on the cross. As a one-off-event with eternal, natural and spiritual consequences, there has never been, nor will there ever need to be, another event like it.

In describing this extraordinary event, the New Testament writers, inspired by the Holy Spirit, found a number of accessible metaphors to describe what Jesus had accomplished. These word pictures would have been readily understood within the culture of the day. Many of these images of the cross come together in Romans 3:23-25:

"For all have sinned and fall short of the glory of God, and are *justified* by his grace as a gift, through the *redemption* that is in Christ Jesus, whom God put forward as a *propitiation by his blood*, to be received by faith. This was to *show God's righteousness*, because in his divine forbearance he had passed over former sins."

Let's look at these pictures in the order Paul mentions them.

## At Calvary We Are Justified

One of the lies which keep us believing that we're separated from God is the lie of shame. This tells us we are unworthy to come close to God, we have to hide, we're unclean, unacceptable, rejected and worthy of perpetual punishment.

To understand why this is a lie we need to understand the difference between guilt and shame.

The Bible starts with the assertion that God created us in His image, and that He made us very good. However, our rebellion, caused by us believing the lies of the enemy, caused us to fall short of the glory of God.

Through dying on the cross, Jesus took our sins upon Himself and put them to death. Thus He declares our sins to be void when we receive His forgiveness, which in legal terms means we are "justified" – "just as if I'd never sinned!" We are no longer guilty sinners; we are beloved children. We need to recognise our sin in order to repent and receive forgiveness, but once it's gone, it's gone!

My understanding of the difference between guilt and shame is as follows: 'guilty' is a factual statement describing someone who has committed an offence. It's a legal state based on what I've done and a judgement from someone in authority, according to an established code of law.

'Shame' is not so much a statement about what I've done but a statement of who I am. It is a description of how I feel about myself as a result of what I've done. It is a cluster of negative emotions in which I see myself as worthless, unlovable, insignificant, dirty, and humiliated. It is a state of being that generates feelings of exile and exclusion, which of course is the fertile soil in which the weeds of hollow religion can grow.

But here's the Good News.

When Jesus died on the cross, He took away not only our guilt but our shame.

The Gospel story is that we were...

1. Made in God's image
2. We rebelled against God
3. God's image in us was marred
4. We became guilty and ashamed
5. Religion couldn't solve this
6. So God in Christ came to earth
7. He died on the cross for our sakes
8. We are now reconciled to the Father

9. We are declared not guilty in heaven

10. We can live as honoured children of God on earth

Now by any standards that's an epic story with a truly redemptive arc. It is Gospel – Good News!

To believe that my sin now separates me from God is therefore to believe a lie. To carry guilt and shame indicates that our emotions are stuck in the problem stage of the story, rather than revelling in the resolution stage.

In the 2002 film version of the Count of Monte Cristo, having escaped from prison and bought himself the title of Count, the lead character Edmond Dantes lives in a palace. But at night he rolls off his luxurious silk-lined bed and sleeps on the cold stone floor. Why does he do this? It is because he cannot believe that he is no longer a prisoner and is now living as a prince. His external circumstances have changed but his internal responses have not. In his heart he is still living in the old part of his story.

Many Christians live like this. We live as if we are still imprisoned by guilt and shame, far away from the palace. A great deal of religious activity is then motivated by a sense of shame. We attempt to impress God with our efforts and actions. These are designed to cover up our sense that we're unworthy, or prove to others that we are of value. In doing this we substitute position for performance. Instead of believing that we are princes and princesses, worthy of the King's love (our position), we believe that we are prisoners and slaves and whip ourselves to earn his favour (our performance).

The truth is we are valuable because God has said so. Nothing we do can add to that. As we learn to ignore the lies of shame and displace them with the truth that we are loved and accepted, the motives for religious activity dry up.

I have a friend, who with her husband, felt that God was leading them as a family to move churches. In the move, God spoke to her and said: "No baking; I don't want you to find your identity in baking any longer." In their previous church she had been known for her gift of baking. Every church event, every new baby, every person in distress, she would bake for them. Of course most baking isn't hollow and religious but for her it had become just that. She recognised that it was her motives that counted. So for her it was to be no more baking when she and her family moved to a new church.

In the early months the shift was painful; she had to build relationships without the gift she'd always used – giving away cakes. After three years of God moving wonderfully in her life, bringing new freedom and security, God removed the ban on baking (much to the delight of her new church family!). She had been hiding behind religious activity but God led her out into greater freedom and deeper relationship.

Whenever we live out of our position rather than performance, we move from religion to relationship and from shame to significance. If we remain in performance-based religion, our sense of shame will give birth to judgemental attitudes and generate a culture of criticism. Shame causes us to be unduly self-conscious and sin-conscious. Shame causes us to link our sin with pain and punishment. A person who feels constantly ashamed will often go to great extents to avoid sin (or to hide sin) because they find the recognition of sin to be profoundly painful. They will also become judgmental about others.

When our goal in life is to attempt to live in religious perfection by avoiding all sins, we can quickly become judgmental or intolerant when others fail in the standards we're trying so hard to achieve ourselves. When we live under the lies of condemnation, we become excessively sin-conscious. A common coping mechanism used to handle this painful burden is to become preoccupied with sin, borrowing the weapons of condemnation that the accuser offers us, first to attack ourselves and then in turn to attack others.

This results in a constant attitude of comparison. Those who are stuck in self-condemnation find unhealthy relief through comparing themselves with someone more sinful and highlighting their mistakes. That gives them a sense of justification or superiority, or simply distracts them from their own shame. Whenever this type of behaviour occurs it reveals a lack of understanding of the great gift of justification.

The truth is that we have all been justified through the death of Jesus. We are no longer guilty and therefore no longer need to feel ashamed. Our attempts to save ourselves, to earn God's acceptance, are so rooted in us that fully embracing this truth in our hearts can be very challenging.

In my own life, I've made it a daily discipline to remind myself of this truth whenever I settle down to meet with God. For so many years I've spent so much time feeling distant, dirty and despairing, under a cloud of shame. I've wasted so much quality time with God by wallowing in the pit of my own sin and missing the truth of how He has washed and accepted me.

The Good News is we are justified. When we put our trust in the finished work of the cross, we are set free from guilt and shame. We are then set free from the religious activity that arises from shame, all of which is a hollow attempt to anaesthetise the pain which shame causes us.

Praise God that through the cross we are justified!

## At Calvary We Are Redeemed

In Romans 3:24, Paul talks about how we are justified "through the redemption that is in Christ Jesus."

In a slave market in the Roman Empire, human beings were traded as commodities. Slaves had no rights and no freedom; they were dehumanised. At certain times men and women of compassion would buy a slave and then grant them their freedom. This is what is meant by redemption. To redeem a slave is literally to buy them out of slavery, to pay the price for their liberation.

Jesus did this for us on the cross. We were enslaved by the enemy because of our sin. Our rebellion against God had sold us into slavery and this slavery is manifested in our addictions, fears, death, powerlessness and being controlled. We were slaves to sin and in the grip of the enemy.

The Jewish writers of the New Testament lived in a world familiar with slavery. They lived in the great story of God's deliverance of them from slavery in Egypt (the Exodus). When using slavery as an explanation of what Jesus achieved on the cross there were at least two meanings for them. The first was that all human beings are hired workers, bought and sold, and restricted to work for others, with no rights. Like the Hebrew slaves in Egypt, we are oppressed and downtrodden. However, God has stepped in to set us free, just as He did in Moses' day. Just as He led the Hebrew people through the Red Sea to the Promised Land, so He has led us through the waters of baptism to a new freedom in the Kingdom of Heaven. As in the Exodus, we have been redeemed!

A slave cannot earn his freedom or an inheritance, however hard he works – however much she pleases her master or is diligent. Slaves remain powerless to buy their freedom through works and wages; they remain at the mercy of their owner and only unmerited generosity from another can bring them freedom. A liberated child of God does not need to earn his freedom through works and wages. A son doesn't need to work hard to earn inheritance from his father. It is given freely. This is why Paul says in Galatians 4:6-7:

"Because you are sons, God has sent the Spirit of his Son into our hearts, crying, 'Abba! Father!' So you are no longer a slave, but a son, and if a son, then an heir through God."

So the wonderful truth of redemption is that on the cross Jesus has done for us what we could not do for ourselves. He has stepped in and paid the price for our freedom, giving us a great inheritance that we did not deserve. Thanks to His death on the cross, we have exchanged slavery for sonship! Out of gratitude for His amazing grace, we pledge ourselves to serving Him for the rest of our days. Having been rescued and redeemed, we choose willingly to follow the One who has paid our ransom price and set us free!

When we make the choice of total submission to our Lord, we bow the knee and make a covenant to follow His example by living a life of service. This is a choice we are offered as His children, invited to serve in His family business. This means that we go from being involuntary slaves to becoming voluntary servants. Slaves have no freedom and are forced to work by coercion and fear. Servants are free people who have chosen to serve, to act in a way that blesses their Master, Jesus.

What drives slaves? What motivates and stimulates them into action? They cannot earn anything. They cannot shape their future destiny or influence others except other slaves around them. They are controlled by whoever owns them and motivated by fear and punishment. Living as a slave results in a profoundly selfish existence because a slave has limited power to help others. Their goal is to protect themselves from punishment or abuse. Their only interaction with their master is through acts of service.

Slaves live at a distance, trying to avoid the pain of "not measuring up" and "getting it wrong."

Prayer, worship, practical service, evangelism, showing mercy, financial giving and all other "Christian" activities, if motivated by the fear of punishment, can become acts of enforced slavery rather than acts of loving service. When this happens they have become acts of hollow religion.

Jesus died to purchase our freedom from slavery. He did this so that we could be reconciled to Him, enjoying close relationship with Him – a relationship in which we are secure in His love, released from control, given an inheritance and invited to serve in the family business. Once again we see how through His death on the cross, Jesus sets us free from hollow religion.

## At Calvary we are Forgiven

The next metaphor used in Romans 3:23-25 to describe what Jesus did on the cross is that of sacrifice. Paul declares:

"...whom God put forward as a propitiation by his blood, to be received by faith. This was to show God's righteousness, because in his divine forbearance he had passed over former sins."

Notice the word "propitiation" here. The Apostle John also uses this word picture: "In this is love, not that we have loved God but that he loved us and sent his Son to be the propitiation for our sins" (1 John 4:10).

Although blood sacrifices, and the impact they have in the heavenly realms, are widely ignored or misunderstood in modern Western culture, they were an established feature of most if not all cultures of the ancient world and are still recognised in some nations as having spiritual power. To have a truly biblical understanding of this, we need to recognise that blood sacrifices have spiritual impact.

The Greek words hilasterion and hilasmos (from which we get "propitiation") are used twice each in the New Testament and there are thirty eight references to "the blood of Jesus." The blood of Jesus is linked in the Bible to each of the metaphors used to describe what happened on the cross. Jesus' death was a blood sacrifice which bought us freedom, reconciliation, justification and victory over the enemy.

This blood sacrifice made by Jesus on our behalf was "once for all." In other words, it signalled the end of all further blood sacrifices for sin. As the writer of the Letter to the Hebrews puts it, "Jesus has no need, like those high priests, to offer sacrifices daily, first for his own sins and then for those of the people, since he did this once for all when he offered up himself" (Hebrews 7:27).

This "once-for-all" nature of the cross was shocking for the Jews in New Testament times. As the Letter to the Hebrews reveals, at Calvary Christ died as the sacrificial Lamb of God. His sacrifice is the better, superior, final and more perfect way.

Chapters 7-9 of Hebrews explore this in great detail. There is no further need for sacrifices on earth whether to please God, bribe Him, assuage Him, establish covenant connection with Him or pay Him homage. Those are all aspects of Old Covenant religion; they are human actions designed to gain what God has already given us completely through Jesus' death.

The significance of the sacrificial death of Jesus (the Lamb of God who takes away the sin of the world) is that this completely redefines the nature of our relationship with God. Through the cross, God has given us forgiveness, acceptance, inheritance, access to His Presence, provision and protection, once and for all, fully and completely through the death of Jesus. Hallelujah!

This means that any efforts we make to try and earn forgiveness, gain God's favour, manipulate ourselves into His inheritance, bribe our way into His presence, are all futile and religious because they are attempting to earn what has already been bought for us. It means that any prayers or worship or rituals we perform, in the hope that we can gain God's pardon, provision or protection, are at best ridiculous and at worst superstitious because Christ has already paid the price for these on the cross. We simply receive these things by faith and submission to Him as Lord, not through effort or superstitious activity.

The cross has therefore once-and-for-all done away with any need for religion. When we step back into hollow religion we are therefore ignoring what Jesus has done for us, trying to earn it all for ourselves.

This is what makes the Apostle Paul livid when he writes to the Christians in Galatia:

"O foolish Galatians! Who has bewitched you? It was before your eyes that Jesus Christ was publicly portrayed as crucified. Let me ask you only this: Did you receive the Spirit by works of the law or by hearing with faith? Are you so foolish? Having begun by the Spirit, are you now being perfected by the flesh? Did you suffer so many things in vain—if indeed it was in vain? Does he who supplies the Spirit to you and works miracles among you do so by works of the law, or by hearing with faith." (Galatians 3:1–5)

Whenever we step back into trying to earn God's forgiveness, we revert to the slavery of hollow religion and undermine the glorious truth of the Gospel – that thanks to Jesus' sacrificial death, we are pardoned and forgiven, set free from our chains and released to live as the liberated children of God in the Kingdom of Heaven on earth.

## At Calvary We Are Made Right With God

We have seen that hollow religion grows when there is any sense of a gap between us and God. This gap increases when we hide in shame, run in fear or rebel in anger against God.

A final biblical interpretation of Jesus' death that Paul explores in Romans 3 is "the Righteousness of God." There are two aspects of righteousness we need to remember when we think about the cross. The first is our own righteousness, which we cannot earn by our own effort but is given to us freely through God's grace. Then secondly there is God's righteousness - the truth that God's dealings with humanity are just, right and loving.

Let me put it like this. The best way of understanding righteousness is by using the phrase "in the right." According to the Bible, as human beings we cannot earn this status (being in the right before God). We are unrighteous. God, on the other hand, is by nature righteous. He is never in the wrong as we are. He is in the right and therefore the only one who can make us in the right too!

To understand the righteousness of God we need to recognise that many human beings throughout history have consciously or subconsciously chosen to judge God. This is a significant and recurring theme in Jewish theology and a tradition that Paul taps into when explaining the Gospel in his letter to the Romans. He knows full well that people have put God in the dock and declared that He is in the wrong.

Laying aside the question of whether we should judge God or not, the reality is that at many levels people do and on the basis of that judgment they either run towards Him, seeing Him for who He truly is, or run from Him, believing the slanderous lies the enemy breathes about Him.

Jesus' death on the cross is at the heart of the Gospel and in

Romans 1-3 Paul explains both how God is both fully right to judge us for our rebellion against him and therefore utterly and amazingly merciful in His choice to die in our place and take our punishment.

All this deals a decisive blow to the idea of self-righteousness - the idea that we can get right with God and become in the right in His eyes simply through the efforts of the human self. This is the attitude that the elder brother has in the story of the lost son in Luke 15. Seeing the free pardon and welcome that the father gives to the rebellious and returning younger son, he moans, "Look, these many years I have served you and I never disobeyed your command."

This is hollow religion! Those who are self-righteous need to find someone to blame when they experience confusion, disappointment or pain. When God has become little more than an impersonal distant force we've been trying to impress, then we blame Him rather than take responsibility for our own mess. That blame increases the gap between us and God yet further, giving more space for hollow religion to develop.

The Gospel demolishes this. At the cross, God proved that He is not to blame and that we are responsible for our lives. As we are able to recognise our responsibility, and God's stunning generous mercy, then we can run to Him, accept forgiveness and be reconciled.

When we do that, we discover that God is always "in the right", and that we are no longer "in the wrong" because He has declared us "in the right" when we came to the cross and said sorry.

That is Good News!

## No More Hollow Religion

Jesus' death on the cross is the solution to hollow religion at every level. Our shame, slavery, striving and self-righteousness are all demolished by what He's done for us. Take hold of that daily; let all these truths sink into your life more deeply and bring you closer to Him.

The cross isn't decoration; it's transformation.

It isn't a relic; it's reconciliation.

It isn't a subject to be debated but an event to be celebrated.

At the cross I am justified, redeemed, pardoned, and made right with God.

The cross brings an end to hollow religion and a beginning to heavenly relationship.

It is a bridge not a badge.

## Notes

i. Timothy Keller Center Church p30-31

# 9

# Resurrection Not Religion

Jesus' death bridged the gap between us and God and brought an end to the lie about God's distance from us for those who truly believe.

This is the Good News of the cross.

But there's more! In fact, there's always more for those who have moved from hollow religion to an authentic relationship with Jesus Christ.

On Easter Sunday, the Son of God rose from the dead!

For those who have eyes to see, the resurrection of Jesus changes everything. When the Father sent the power of the Holy Spirit into the tomb of His dead Son, this grave-busting power didn't just transform the body of Jesus. It also marked a brand new beginning for the planet.

This is one of the things that hollow religion cannot and will never understand. Only those who have experienced the same power that raised Jesus from the dead can access such an epic view of the resurrection. For them, Easter Sunday can never be a matter of religious form. It is a matter of resurrection power. Jesus didn't rise from the dead merely to start a new religion; he did it to turn around the whole of creation from decay to hope, from death to new life.

## Victory over Death

In the last chapter we looked at some of the metaphors used in the New Testament to describe the effects of the cross. In this chapter there is another metaphor we need to consider – one that embraces both Jesus' death and resurrection. This is the truth of victory over the powers of darkness.

Here are some references to this idea of Christ's victory:

"Through death he might destroy the one who has the power of death, that is, the devil." (Hebrews 2:14)

"The reason the Son of God appeared was to destroy the works of the devil." (1 John 3:8)

"He disarmed the rulers and authorities and put them to open shame, by triumphing over them in him." (Colossians 2:15)

What these passages are pointing to is the fact that through His death and resurrection Jesus defeated Satan and the forces of evil. This includes the demonic scheme to sterilise the church with hollow religion.

This is something we find throughout the New Testament. Christ's death and resurrection bring about a victory over the accuser, the power of death, and over the rulers and authorities in the heavenly realms. This victory was achieved through both the devastation of Good Friday and the recreation of Easter Sunday. Thanks to both these events, God has intervened to rescue us from the dominion of darkness and bring us into the kingdom of the Son He loves. This victory demolishes the power that sin and death had over us, the control they had through condemnation, slavery, deception and indeed hollow religion, through which the enemy seeks to control and restrict us.

This victory over every work of Satan and his demonic forces means that we can live in victory over hollow religion. Jesus came to seek and save those who were lost in immorality and those who were lost in hollow religion, by reconciling us to the Father as his much loved adopted sons and daughters. He has defeated both of the schemes (slavery to sin and slavery to religion) designed by the evil one to keep us from living a fulfilled kingdom life. He has done this by paving a way back to the Father's house in heaven, enabling many sons and daughters to enjoy the glorious presence of the Father.

## Three Great Gifts

In his letter to the Ephesians, Paul includes two stunning prayers which he prays for the believers in Ephesus. In the first, in chapter 1, he prays that they might have the spirit of wisdom and revelation to know:
- The hope to which God has called them
- The riches of his glorious inheritance
- The power of God at work towards/for us who believe.

Let's look at these three.

First of all, hope bursts into bloom wherever the reality of the resurrection takes root. That Sunday morning when Jesus defeated death, everything changed. The dismal, grey, frightening, empty future His followers feared was suddenly transformed into vibrant expectation. In short, hope was reborn.

The moment we accept Jesus as Lord, and enter into covenant relationship with him, joy becomes part of our present and hope shapes our future. We have the promise of the Father's provision and protection and the joy of His presence to look forward to, with the assurance of eternal life.

Secondly, none of this can be earned as wages through hollow religious effort. The hope born of religion is a worldly hope, an insecure wondering if we've done enough, an empty hope that we might get lucky and be blessed. But resurrection hope is solid and dependable; it is the hope of an indescribably rich inheritance! As Peter says,

"According to his great mercy, he has caused us to be born again to a living hope through the resurrection of Jesus Christ from the dead, to an inheritance that is imperishable, undefiled, and unfading, kept in heaven for you, who by God's power are being guarded through faith for a salvation ready to be revealed in the last time. In this you rejoice, though now for a little while, if necessary, you have been grieved by various trials." (1 Peter 1:3-6)

Our inheritance is "imperishable … kept in heaven for you."

This gives us a wonderful security in this life because we know we can't waste our inheritance away now; it will never run out.

Hollow religion is an attempt to hold onto what we've worked for. If we see God's favour as something that we've had to strive for through discipline, morality and good deeds, then we'll see it as a retirement fund, a pension that we've earned through life which we need to protect. Any such limited thinking will cause us to live life in a way that is defensive and backward-looking. But our security isn't found in what we've earned but what we've received. Just as we didn't earn it ourselves, so we cannot squander it ourselves.

The prodigal son spent his inheritance and then, when reconciled to his father, he received a fresh inheritance - the best robe, the family signet ring and some luxury leather shoes. Although he returned home expecting to have to earn his food and shelter, he discovered that home is a place of undeserved abundance. This is our security: that wherever we wander, however we rebel, whenever we fail, we have a home.

As the quotation from 1 Peter shows, resurrection hope gives us a security through trials, pain and persecution. The history of persecution and martyrdom is a sobering and challenging reminder that persecution refines us. The empty chaff of self-reliance is quickly burned away but those who endure are those who are rooted in this hope.

In the midst of persecution, hollow religion becomes defensive and more rigid. But in the midst of persecution, resurrection hope shines brighter, more clearly, more beautifully, through the refining fire. From Stephen in Acts 8, to the many Christians still experiencing persecution around the world today, there is a rich history of God's children facing torture and death with hope and joy, as they look to their true home.

But there's more!

The resurrection of Jesus is thirdly the greatest demonstration of God's power. Until Jesus rose from the grave, the most potent force on earth was death. But then Jesus defeated it. On Easter Sunday He proved that there is a power greater than death and that power is resurrection life.

In describing the power of God for us, Paul talks about "the immeasurable greatness of his power toward us who believe, according to the working of his great might that he worked in Christ when he raised him from the dead and seated him at his right hand in the heavenly places" (Ephesians 1:19–20).

Notice the piling up of power words here - power, working, great might, and worked. It's as if Paul is straining the resources of finite human language to describe this limitless, infinite resurrection power.

The resurrection is the greatest demonstration of God's power. If we long for the Kingdom of God and to see His power at work in our lives, rather than a mere religious form of godliness, then our understanding of the power of God will be defined by the power of the resurrection.

This power is for us!

This is really important when we consider the remark in 2 Timothy 3.5 about "having a form of godliness, but denying its power." The supernatural power of God is the core of the Christian life. It is not only the power that raised Jesus from death (and therefore at the core of Christian faith) it is also the life-giving power at work within every true believer (and therefore the core of the Christian life). Hollow religion isn't therefore a substandard pale reflection of Kingdom living; it is a denial of God's supernatural grace at work in us and a denial of the one thing that causes Christianity to stand out from all other faiths on the earth – the resurrection of Jesus.

## From Form to Power

Thanks to the resurrection of Christ, we can expect God to move powerfully now. It is the ultimate miracle both because it defies all previous human experiences of death (where death is a hopeless end) and because it opens up the reality of an open heaven for us now (offering us an endless hope).

Hollow religion attempts to live out Christian faith (or any other religious faith) without miracles, signs and wonders - in short, without evidences of resurrection power. This isn't just a dim reflection of what we see in the Gospels; it's a denial of all that Jesus modelled for us about His kingdom.

There are whole swathes of the Gospel which are flooded with miracles, signs and wonders: the birth narratives where King Jesus is born; His early ministry in Galilee, when He announces His kingdom; and after His resurrection when He demonstrates His kingdom breaking into the present age.

It is interesting to note that the miracles after the resurrection seem to have a different tone from those before. Jesus walks through walls, hides his identity and then discloses it; He cooks fish on a beach when we know the local fisherman hadn't been able to catch any.

The miracles at his birth were primarily angelic announcements of life overcoming sterility. The miracles which accompany the announcement of His Kingdom in His ministry on earth were mainly healing and deliverance miracles – signs pointing to His glorious divinity. The miracles after the resurrection demonstrate a whole new order of being. From now on the established norms and laws don't seem to apply to Jesus.

The resurrection redefines what is normal, giving us a "new normal" in which we are not mere mortals bound to a merely natural, safe existence but people in whom the death-defeating power of the Holy Spirit lives!

This means once again that there is so much more!

Hollow religion seeks to make the church safe and understandable to the world around us. In doing this, the Church is infiltrated and debilitated by the world's thinking. That is not the new normal that Jesus has made available to us.

## Dynamic Resurrection Life

The climax of C.S. Lewis' The Lion, the Witch and the Wardrobe comes when Aslan, the lion who represents Christ, rises from the dead having been killed in place of the boy Edmund who has betrayed him. As Edmund's two sisters go to the stone table where Aslan was brutally murdered, they meet the risen lion. He explains what has happened. He talks about an even deeper magic that the wicked Queen did not know, one in which "even death itself will turn backwards."

The resurrection is the great turning point of history, the great reversal of the process of decay, which started with man's rebellion in the garden. When Jesus rose from the dead, the recreation of the earth began. Those who have renounced hollow religion for resurrection power live in this reality, this deeper magic in which death itself turns backwards. So it is that Paul declares in Romans 8:21, "The creation itself will be liberated from its bondage to decay and brought into the freedom and glory of the children of God."

From the Fall of humankind in the Garden of Eden, creation became subject to decay – to a slow, gradual disintegration and to what is known as atrophy. Any living thing separated from its source of life becomes dry or mouldy and decomposes. Human effort, engineering, building, restoration, has done all it can to see progress. Civilisations have grown and scientific knowledge has advanced. Yet people, plants and animals keep dying and decay is an accepted norm.

However, something seismic has changed all this. On Easter Sunday, tectonic plates began to shift. A brave new world began to emerge. God in Christ started to make all things new in the midst of this decaying world. He caused death to start working backwards and initiated a process which is working in the opposite direction of atrophy and decay to this day.

In 1 Corinthians 15, Paul discusses the resurrection of Christ. In part of this he writes about a contrast between perishable and imperishable: "I tell you this, brothers and sisters: flesh and blood cannot inherit the kingdom of God, nor does the perishable inherit the imperishable ... For this perishable body must put on the imperishable, and this mortal body must put on immortality. When the perishable puts on the imperishable, and the mortal puts on immortality, then shall come to pass the saying that is written: 'Death is swallowed up in victory'" (1 Corinthians 15:50; 53–54). What great news this is! We no longer need to live out of a fear of perpetual decay. We can live convinced that death itself is working backwards and that the cry from heaven is, "Behold, I am making all things new!"

## A Brand New Mindset

One day I was cycling to meet my wife Nells at the hospital for the twenty week scan of our third son. At breakfast that morning she had asked me, "Have you decided yet?" For weeks I had been postponing the decision whether we would find out the gender. A friend of ours, a radiographer, was working that day at the hospital and she'd arranged to do the scan. Nells wanted to find out the baby's gender but I was still resistant. As I cycled, I still hadn't decided and I only had five minutes left. Suddenly a thought hit me so forcefully that I can still point to the exact turning in the street where it struck me: "Given that Jesus was a radical, who came to change the world and challenge the status quo, why is the church renowned for being static and attempting to conserve things from the past?"

That was my decision made for me! My only reason at the time for not wanting to know the gender was that it wasn't the "traditional" thing to do.

That represented the exact opposite of the way of thinking that God was encouraging me to embrace. Hollow religion is attracted to the static and traditional. This is why Jesus rebuked the Pharisees, saying, "For the sake of your tradition you have made void the word of God" (Matthew 15:6). Paul warned, "See to it that no one takes you captive by philosophy and empty deceit, according to human tradition, according to the elemental spirits of the world, and not according to Christ" (Colossians 2:8).

Some traditions can have value. Under the Old Covenant God commanded certain traditions for the sake of remembering His acts of love and power. Under the New Covenant, Jesus instructed us to share communion (a living tradition) and Paul used the word "tradition" in a positive way in 2 Thessalonians. Traditions which are done in obedience to God do not make the Word of God void, nor will they take us captive and have control over us. However, when hollow religion takes hold of traditions and sucks the life our of them, they can be turned against God's Kingdom purposes.

Hollow religion places huge emphasis on tradition for two reasons. Firstly, traditions are saturated in knowledge and empower those who have that knowledge to raise themselves above others, usually in an attitude of criticism and judgement. We see examples of this in Matthew 15, Romans 14, Colossians 2 and 1 Corinthians 8.

Secondly traditions are comfortable. I love chutney and one of my favourite producers is a company called 'Preserving Traditions'. Their marketing consciously emphasises traditional recipes and methods of chutney production. They know that every form of marketing appeals to basic attractions and desires. The reason why hollow tradition markets itself effectively is because human beings are attracted to the comfort of familiarity.

In Matthew 25 Jesus tells the parable of the talents. A master goes away on a journey, entrusting portions of his property to three servants. The first two servants trade with their talents and through adventure, action and movement, double their employer's money. The third, through fear, hides the talent in the ground and earns nothing except his master's extreme displeasure.

Notice here the contrast between being dynamic and static. The first two servants are dynamic; the third is static. Living from a centre of fear, he avoids risk taking and seeks the safety of inactivity, thereby revealing an attitude that is the furthest remove from the Kingdom Jesus came to establish – a Kingdom of change, growth and movement.

## New Creations

Political commentator Andrew Sullivan says "All conservatism begins with loss."[i] Faced with secularisation in the Western world, particularly in the area of ethics, the Church has reacted with a conservatism which at times focuses on fearing what we're losing rather than hoping for what God is going to do.

In the UK we often try to restore a perceived golden era of being a Christian nation, when Church attendance was high, morality strict and Christianity respected. But what if what we are seeking to restore was not an era of genuine openness to salvation, submission to God and Kingdom life? What if the golden era of high numbers in Church was merely hollow religion?

One residue of this hollow religion is seen in the fact that often in my social context I become a kind of guilt trigger to others. Chatting to people in the street, they will often apologise for not attending Church more often. This highlights to me that under hollow religion, attendance numbers were often high because people were afraid of censure by others not because they were filled with resurrection life.

The Kingdom of God is not a response to decay; it is a celebration of resurrection life. That being the case I believe we should not be characterised by a defence of traditions, designed as levies against the tides of change. Rather we should be characterised as a people who live in the power of the resurrection and believe we are dynamic new creations in the midst of the old.

## Jesus is Alive!

The final way in which the resurrection demolishes hollow religion is through the great truth declared across the world on Easter Sunday, "Jesus is alive!"

We know, love and serve a risen Saviour. He is there when we talk to Him. He is forever at the right hand of the Father, preparing an eternal home for us. It's so simple but wonderfully true.

If Jesus had simply died then like many other religions all we would have now would be a movement to preserve His teaching and celebrate His legacy. But we have so much more; we have a risen Saviour whom we can know today and look forward to getting to know better in the future, both on earth and in heaven. This glorious truth reshapes everything, including intercessory prayer. Hebrews 7:25 tells us that Jesus lives to make intercession for us. I don't read this as a religious form of intercessory prayer but that in heaven Jesus is before the Father as our advocate, bringing our requests to the Father as mediator. In this way He is the complete opposite of Satan who attempts to accuse humans before God.

Likewise, the great truth that Jesus is alive reshapes the way we pray as we seek to bring heaven to earth. When we pray, we are longing for more of what we've already seen Jesus do. We are saying to God, "I want more of heaven on earth right now because I know you are good and I know you can." Our intercessory prayer is built on relationship and fuelled by hope.

By contrast, when hollow religion starts to shape intercessory prayer it becomes lost in the lie that we have to strive on earth to get prayer right, in the hope that we'll persuade a distant God to respond. Any prayer which is not built around relational interaction with the Father and Son, through the Spirit, can become a hollow religious exercise.

Hollow intercession is tedious, heavy and even superstitious, all of which puts us off and prevents us engaging in the cooperation God calls us to, restoring His world.

First of all it is tedious.

Hollow intercession becomes an obligation. Although we might try and mix it up and make it fun, unless prayer is an activity in which heaven and earth connect supernaturally then it becomes dull and little more than information sharing.

A friend of mine, working for a missions agency, once described her team's weekly prayer meeting as "Going around the world sharing information and reminding God about situations He was already aware of as a nice gesture of love to those there. There was not an ounce of faith in the room that anything we did could change anything on the ground."

Secondly, it is heavy.

When intercessory prayer becomes motivated by a fear of judgement and disaster, then it quickly becomes a burden. In such a context of prayer, we become the saviours approaching a God of anger to appease Him. Under the New Covenant, however, Jesus' death on the cross and His sending of the Holy Spirit reshape our model of prayer. Prayer is now seen as partnering with God to see on earth the victory Jesus has already won for us. We take on His prayer burden, which is light, His prayer yoke which is easy.

Thirdly, hollow intercession can become superstitious.

Intercession can easily be hijacked by principles, techniques or formulae. Applying certain principles and techniques, with no expectation of the steering of the Holy Spirit, is close to superstition.

Intercessory prayer is, by its nature, a supernatural activity, based in the reality of the resurrection. Our words in the natural realm have an influence on the heavenly realms. As members of

God's Kingdom, the only legitimate source of information we have into the heavenly realms is revelation from the Holy Spirit. The simple application of techniques or principles in intercession, without submission and listening to the Holy Spirit, makes intercession a hollow and superstitious activity.

## An Easter Sunday Faith

"I will hope continually" David cries in Psalm 71:14. We are called to continual hope. By its very nature, hope like this will continue to experience joys and breakthroughs even in time of persecution and pressure. As the longed for future vision becomes our reality, continual hope stretches out for more, longs for more, prays for more and expects in faith to see it.

When we consider the deep and wonderful truths of what Jesus achieved for us through his resurrection, we see such amazing revelation of the character of God and the dynamics of His Kingdom. We see the grace of God in breaking into a decaying world. We see the power of God in defeating death and creating new life. We see the love of God in accepting us as His children and giving us an inheritance. We see that God's ways are creative and dynamic and bursting with hope and we see that God has made a way for us to be reconciled to Him, rather than living isolated from Him.

Truly, the resurrection changes everything.

## Notes

i. Andrew Sullivan, *The Conservative Soul*, p9.

# 10
# Filled With the Spirit

Earlier in this book I talked about the importance of exhaling the green mist of religion from our lungs. Once this happens, the empty space left by the toxic power of hollow religion needs to be filled with something altogether more whole and holy, namely the Spirit of God. Once we have expelled the foul air, we need to inhale fresh air – the breath and wind of God's Holy and life-giving Spirit.

All this highlights the fact that the process of getting free from religion requires that we take a number of distinct steps from our lethargic and diseased spiritual state:

1. Wake Up: we need to wake up to the fact that we have been rendered dormant by hollow religion.

2. Rise Up: we need to break out of the paralysis of passivity and become resolved to choose life and freedom.

3. Cough Up: we need to receive deliverance from all traces of hollow and deadening religion.

4. Look Up: we need to move from religious worship (God is distant) to relational worship (God is our loving Dad).

5. Fill Up: we need to go on being filled with the power that

raised Jesus from the dead – the Holy Spirit.

Perhaps nowhere is the difference between hollow religion and heavenly relationship more accentuated than in the matter of being filled with the Holy Spirit. In hollow religion, the experiential reality of being supernaturally infused with the power of heaven is an alien concept. Built as it is on the lie of God's distance, hollow religion makes no room for encounter because encounter implies nearness where religion prefers remoteness. To be filled with the Spirit means to be wrecked, ravaged and intoxicated by the love of God. Hollow religion is allergic to such intimacy.

When a person is filled with the Spirit they are experiencing nothing less than what the Bible knows as the normal Christian life. When the Spirit fills us, the unseen Spirit of God impacts our physical bodies in such a way that we are transformed. From the moment of this tangible experience we live differently, from a centre of love as opposed to fear. The Spirit of God is therefore the missing ingredient in hollow religion. Those who privilege religion over relationship cannot understand this; perfect love has not yet cast out fear in them (1 John 4:18).

When we seek to understand the Holy Spirit our minds are stretched because God has revealed His Spirit to be both a person of the Trinity – God Himself – and also a dynamic, unseen, spiritual force. This remains a mystery and keeps us from ever attempting to believe that we can constrain or control God. The richest and clearest term I have come across to describe the Holy Spirit is Gordon Fee's "God's Empowering Presence." But even this cannot be said to be the final word. God's Spirit is a tornado that we cannot contain!

All this gives no grounds for the religious person to call the Holy Spirit a mystery and leave it at that, as if a mysterious person can never be encountered in love! The Holy Spirit does not legitimate the hollow religious life because the Holy Spirit is the "unreligious spirit". That is not to say that the Holy Spirit must be defined by what He is against. He is so much more than merely the opposite of the religious spirit although He emphatically is the antithesis of those demonic spirits which seek to constrain God's people in hollow religion.

If we take the contrasts I mentioned earlier in this book between hollow religion and Kingdom life we can see this clearly. In chapter 1 I talked about hollow religion as form not power, knowledge not revelation, judgement not grace, static not dynamic, and about wages not inheritance. As we celebrate the Spirit-filled, Kingdom life, we see these contrasts in reverse.

## Power Not Form

Hollow religion is preoccupied with appearance, with outward form, with what things look like, with things that are seen. The Holy Spirit however is unseen. If you want to build a church by appealing to those who are impressed by physical form – the aesthetics of architecture and ritual – then inviting the Spirit to work amongst you is unlikely to be a primary focus. If however you want to build a church that is alive to God and seeing demonstrations of God's power and love in its community, then welcoming the Spirit of God is likely to be your priority and indeed your passion.

Right now you are reading a book. This book is full of ideas and beliefs – I hope most of them revealed by the Holy Spirit and based on the Bible, another book full of stories and concepts and creeds. This shows that we cannot avoid the fact that there is a proportion of Christianity that is abstract and conceptual, full of ideas, values and principles. None of this is to be despised or rejected.

However, when we prioritise a cognitive, intellectual faith over an affectionate, passionate one we are likely to find ourselves becoming more and more sceptical and ineffective. When we doubt, it is usually in our heads. Our minds question, think through and ponder different approaches to life and experience from those that have been rooted in biblical faith. These can then be discussed or debated with no impact on our actual lives. Doubt is usually conceptual long before it shapes our actions or choices. For those who have hollow religion but no heavenly relationship, doubts are usually hidden by shame and toxic to the heart, they slowly undermine the edifice of an intellectual faith. When we live in heavenly relationship with God, doubts come and go, but we take them to our loving Heavenly Father and in that relationship, we welcome the Holy Spirit to guide us into deeper roots in truth. While the Holy Spirit is unseen, He is also tangible and real and impacts the physical realm. The power of God heals bodies, multiplies food, stirs emotions and reveals things to the mind and imagination that could not naturally be known by reading or listening to others speak.

All of these things happened when the power of the Spirit impacted human beings in the Bible. These experiences were the result of the power of God invading the natural realm and bringing change. From this moment on, the unseen power of God was the priority, not visible form.

If you take a panoramic view of the global church in the 21st century, where the Church is embracing the power of God – praying for healings, signs, wonders and demonstrations of God's power - and demonstrating God's love and mercy through feeding the poor and caring for the vulnerable, it is growing exponentially. Where the church has focussed on debate, ideas, intellectual theology, it is shrinking in numbers and influence, meandering into cul-de-sacs of irrelevance.

Many people in the world today are no longer asking 'Is it true?' but 'Is it authentic?' A Christianity of knowledge, rules and outward form will become increasingly obsolete and marginalised. On the other hand, a Christianity in which the reality of God's power, expressed through supernatural signs and wonders and demonstrations of sacrificial love and selfless generosity, will enjoy the opposite destiny; it will point a bewildered world to the reality of Jesus.

Many of us live in a context where miracles are few and experiences of God's power are rare. Hollow religion accepts that and builds carefully formed and controlled projects and doctrines to justify a theology of absence and distance. But the heart-cry of a Spirit-filled church is "Come, Lord Jesus. We want more. We long for earth to be more like heaven."

This kind of cry can only happen by the power of the Holy Spirit, not through human effort or worldly wisdom. One of the first signs of hearts becoming open to the Holy Spirit is a deep cry to see more of God's manifest presence and less human striving. This is the cry for power over form.

## Revelation Not Knowledge

I believe it is impossible to break away from hollow religion without learning to live by revelation. If hollow religion is defined as Christianity at a distance from God, then the only remedy for hollow religion is to live by the daily bread of His revelation. Man-made, academic, theological knowledge is not enough. We need the Holy Spirit to speak to our hearts not just academics to speak to our heads.

John Eldredge puts this brilliantly:

"If you're not pursuing a dangerous quest with your life, well, then you don't need a Guide. If you haven't found yourself in the midst of a ferocious war, then you won't need a seasoned Captain. If you've settled in your mind to live as though this is a fairly neutral world and you are simply trying to live your life as best you can, then you can probably get by with the Christianity of tips and techniques. Maybe. I'll give you about a fifty-fifty chance. But if you intend to live in the story that God is telling, and if you want the life he offers, then you are going to need more than a handful of principles, however noble they may be. There are too many twists and turns in the road ahead, too many ambushes waiting only God knows where, too much at stake. You cannot possibly prepare yourself for every situation. Narrow is the way said Jesus. How shall we be sure to find it? We need God intimately, we need him desperately."[i]

The wonderful news is that God has provided a seasoned captain to walk alongside us, guide us, instruct us and empower us. As Jesus said to his disciples:

"I will ask the Father, and he will give you another Helper, to be with you forever, even the Spirit of truth, whom the world cannot receive, because it neither sees him nor knows him. You know him, for he dwells with you and will be in you... I will not leave you as orphans; I will come to you." (John 14:16–18)

The Holy Spirit is our helper and Jesus promised to send him to us. The Greek word translated helper is parakletos, which has provoked a great deal of discussion. The literal meaning is "one who comes alongside us."

When Jesus returned to heaven, having completed his mission to reconcile us to the Father and defeat death, He didn't want us to remain at a distance from God. He didn't want His leaving to create a gap which we would fill with religion. So He promised to send His Spirit and then fulfilled that promise dramatically on the

Day of Pentecost.

The Holy Spirit brings us revelation from heaven. He gives the gift of prophecy. He opens our eyes to see visions. He speaks to us. I've discovered that all this boils down to a simple matter of faith. I need to choose to believe whether God will speak to me or not. When God turned my life around in 2004, one of the first areas that changed was my faith to believe that I could hear His voice. At the time my expectations were low. I had the occasional picture at special events or on retreat but I didn't expect my Father to speak to me daily. Being plunged into a culture where everyone expected God to speak to them completely redefined what is normal. I longed for more and started to practise and believe. I found simple, safe, easy places to listen to God. I learned to ask God the right questions.

"When you made this person, what are some of the things that you made special about them?"

"What is your design for this church service, Lord?"

"What is the enemy attempting to do here to hinder your Kingdom?"

"Where are the things in my life that are not aligned to your Kingdom and that are hindering me from living fully what you've called me to?"

I found praying for others and daring to ask God for words of encouragement for them became easier and easier. I've not found anyone who objects to hearing a word of encouragement. I've led churches with the assumption that all of God's children can hear Him speak. We all have the same inheritance - to hear the voice of our Father. This may not yet be the norm in much of the Church in the West, but it is the norm in the Kingdom. All we need to do is create simple, safe contexts for people to "have a go" and learn to hear God's voice.

Recently we held an evening to pray for one another for what we call "Original Design" – a simple model of group prayer for an individual, asking God to reveal prophetically how He made them and specific words to encourage them and reveal to them their true identity. I set up groups led by those who had done this before and invited a new batch of leaders in our church to be prayed for and listen to God for themselves.

As the evening began, after a five minute briefing, I could feel the fear in the room. People were anxious about whether they would "perform" well. Others were analysing and critiquing the model. Others were looking around to work out why they had been put in the group they were in.

After twenty minutes, the atmosphere had completely shifted. God was speaking and people loving it. There was laughter and joyful tears as God spoke deeply to peoples' heart's desires or gave pictures that connected with powerful past memories. Those who had no expectation that they would hear God speak found they had words or pictures for someone else, about things they could never have known.

When the Holy Spirit speaks, He brings life. He brings joy and causes truths to sink deep into our hearts. We need to find appropriate contexts to help this happen – a structure for spontaneity. Form is useful if it is then filled with God's power.

The more I listen, the more I hear. The less pressure I place on myself hearing God, the less tense I am about it and the more I hear. The more I believe that He loves me and wants to speak to me, the more I hear. The less focus I place on myself and the more I make listening to Him about Him, the more I hear.

There is so much to say on this subject. Many other books have been written on hearing God's voice already. All I want to add here is that, as you turn your face to God, fill your lungs with the

Spirit and ask the Lord to speak to you. He will. Like Peter in Acts 10, if you're willing to hear outside the box of your understanding, then you will hear more.

In John 14, Jesus goes on to say: "The Helper, the Holy Spirit, whom the Father will send in my name, he will teach you all things and bring to your remembrance all that I have said to you... Peace I leave with you; my peace I give to you" (John 14:26–27). This is an amazing promise. I can imagine some of the disciples were anxiously trying to remember everything Jesus had taught them after He announced that he was leaving them - scribbling notes, revising key parables, trying to remember key quotes, making mental lists of top tips, trying to remember which beatitudes went with which blessings, wanting to grasp hold of the knowledge they'd need for the task ahead.

Jesus promises them something so much better – the Holy Spirit to teach them all things and remind them what He had taught. That promise is foundational. Jesus promised that the Spirit would remind them of what they would need to know – the right thing for the right occasions.

It gives me great comfort as someone who teaches the Bible that I don't have to cover every topic, test my church with exams or control each member of the church to hear each sermon I preach. That would be an impossible task. So we lean back on the sovereignty of God and the promise that the Holy Spirit is our teacher. He brings the revelation at the right time.

Freedom from hollow religion will come as we choose to trust the Holy Spirit and ask for revelation, rather than trying to store up knowledge for ourselves.

Let's prioritise heavenly revelation over human knowledge.

## Grace Not Judgment

The Holy Spirit is the One who sanctifies us, who washes us clean, who is continually saving us from the decay of our sin, to become more like Jesus. This is a work of grace and a further demonstration of the loving character of a good God. In His kindness, God chose for mercy to triumph over judgement by Jesus dying on the cross. That same process continues as God forgives and restores us by His Spirit, cleansing us and transforming us from deceived rebels into loving heirs.

There are many ways in which this happens. When He is poured out upon us and living within us, the Holy Spirit teaches us to believe the truth of God's grace and empowers us to resist sin and renounce the enemy.

In Romans 5:5 Paul reveals that one way in which the Spirit sanctifies us is through pouring the love of the Father into our hearts: "God's love has been poured into our hearts through the Holy Spirit who has been given to us." It is the Father's affection, affirmation and acceptance that make us holy and make us whole. Everyone I have ever met has to some extent been shaped by rejection. Some of us had loving, secure parents. Others were abused, rejected or abandoned. All of us were brought up by fallen, broken human beings, living in a broken, selfish world. These experiences created a void in our hearts - an emptiness caused by the deprivation of love. Whether rejection has been dramatic and obvious, or relatively mild and minor, it damages our sense of identity and security and this causes us to grab love for ourselves rather than give it away.

The truth of Romans 5:5 is that abandonment and rejection can be healed when we allow the Holy Spirit to pour the Father's love into our hearts. God designed us to live in permanent loving relationship with Him. After Adam and Eve fell, human beings became disconnected from that relationship and from the constant source of love which empowers human beings. Reconciliation with the Father makes it possible once again to be filled with the Father's love and this is the work of the Holy Spirit. This is all part of the amazing gift of God's grace. Like the prodigal son, we have wandered off in rebellion to the far country. When we are reconciled with the Father, He doesn't treat us as our sins deserve. He lavishes love upon us.

Starving orphans grab and grasp at any food which they think will feed them, whether it is healthy or not. Our bodies were designed to be fuelled by food, the healthier the better. When we receive insufficient food, we get hungry or, worse, we starve. Our stomachs send a signal to our hands and mouth, "Feed me! Fill me up NOW!" If we're responsive to that signal, then we grab whatever we can to fill our stomachs, to alleviate the pain of acute hunger.

When our hearts are starved of love, our inner being cries out for acceptance, kindness, encouragement, gentleness and the comfort of being protected and valued. Our emotions send signals to our brain, "Feed me! Fill me up NOW!" Through infancy, childhood and adolescence we learn to grasp at any form of acceptance or comfort in order to fill up the emptiness we feel so acutely inside.

There is great variety in those actions. Some are what can generally be classed as "legitimate" calls for love. Others are "illegitimate". The culture we live in will define which behaviours are legitimate and which are illegitimate. I hope that our church cultures are shaped by clear biblical teaching on legitimate calls for love.

Many of us fish for compliments to earn value and favour. We find relationships where we are valued, affirmed and protected.

We work extremely hard in a professional career or in academic study to gain a sense of significance and self-worth. We shop until we drop, desperately trying to find consumer goods that bring a sense of satisfaction. These are all behaviours that could be called legitimate because they do not directly harm others and so are not regarded as shameful.

But then there are the more obviously dangerous manifestations of a hunger for love – using drugs or alcohol; flirting; dressing in a sexually provocative way; engaging in sexual relationships outside of marriage; pornography; gambling; spending excessively and spiralling into debt; violence; dabbling with occult experiences. These are examples of illegitimate expressions of love hunger, which the Bible defines as disobedience to God.

Hollow religion, as defined in this book, is an activity fuelled by a deep hunger for love. In the absence of the Father's love, poured out open desperate and hungry hearts by the Holy Spirit, we create a religion as a substitute for relationship. No wonder we then become judgmental. In the absence of an encounter with God's lavish grace, we feel judged and fear punishment. This leads to us judging others.

At times in my life when I have felt empty, rejected, criticised and unloved, I know that I have found comfort or distraction from my own pain by criticising and judging others. Judging can bring with it a sense of self-righteousness and, if we are effective in judging others, we can find affirmations of that from other religious people who boost our false sense of superiority that we alone think rightly about God and about the Christian life.

Judging others can make us feel good; it can make us feel free, powerful, right, clever, and superior.

I recently watched a short video clip of a prominent Christian leader judging and criticising another movement within the

Church. His audience were cheering and encouraging him. His rhetoric gathered pace and he became impassioned as he ranted against fellow believers.

As I watched the clip, judgement rose up in me. I felt angry and critical of this leader. I wanted to rant about him on twitter and express my disgust at his abuse of his public voice. Thankfully the Lord has banned me from publicly criticising anyone and so I turned to the Father and brought my sense of injustice to him. As I engaged with the love the Father has for me, the need to criticise, judge, or make a statement faded and was replaced with a desire to forgive, love, bless and pray for this leader. As Peter said of Jesus, "When he was reviled, he did not revile in return; when he suffered, he did not threaten, but continued entrusting himself to him who judges justly" (1 Peter 2:23).

On the cross (which is what this passage in 1 Peter is referring to) Jesus handed the injustice against him to the Father. Part of forgiveness is handing over my perceived right to judge another to God, who is judge of all.

Knowing that we are loved, demolishes the need to judge others, particularly our brothers and sisters in Christ. When we allow the Holy Spirit to fill our hearts with the love of the Father, then our hunger for acceptance and worth from others fades away. When we are filled with the love of the Father, we enjoy blessing and not cursing, honouring and not slandering. We enjoy describing the good things that God and His people are doing - telling stories of kindness, mercy, miracles, joy, new life, salvation. We renounce judgment – enjoying the buzz we get from scoring points or finding agreement with others in attacking the parts of the family business that aren't doing things the way we believe is "right" – and we receive grace!

As the Holy Spirit fills our hearts with the love of the Father, our vision expands and our love for the family expands. We are more able to love and bless and forgive those who disagree with us. The Holy Spirit takes grace beyond just an idea to an experience that transforms us to become those who show grace to others.

## Dynamic Not Static

There are times when you walk into a room and the atmosphere there is just different from the norm.

One evening I went to hear Surprise Sithole. Surprise works with Rolland and Heidi Baker in Mozambique, overseeing the churches in the revival there. He has seen thousands of churches and orphanages planted, lives changed, healings, miracles and people raised from the dead. We had looked forward to the evening and knew it would be a special time.

Sometimes the most profound things are the simplest. Surprise stood up, laughed a bit and then announced in a deep African voice: "It needs to get looser in here!"

There was no judgement or criticism in his voice. He exuded joy and laughter from every pore of his body. He just wanted us to see that for us to encounter all that the Holy Spirit had for us that night we needed to get "looser." You may have no idea what that means. I didn't but my spirit jumped. I listened to him preach and by the end of the evening I had a taste of what he meant.

A few years on, the word "looser" has become very precious to me. I am convinced that as we become looser we give more opportunity for the Holy Spirit to move amongst us. So, sit back and get looser! As Jesus said, "The wind blows where it wishes and you hear its sound, but you do not know where it comes from or where it goes. So it is with everyone born of the Spirit" (John 3:8).

The same Greek word, pneuma, can be translated as wind or

spirit. This means that this verse is often read as being primarily about the Holy Spirit and His dynamic nature. But read it again and focus on the final sentence: "So it is with everyone born of the Spirit."

Jesus makes this point to Nicodemus when speaking about the need to be born again and for us to become spiritual, heavenly people. It's a verse that has intrigued me for the past few years as I've woken up to the importance of becoming less static and more dynamic.

Those who are born of the Spirit are like the Spirit, who is like the wind – constantly moving, having a continuous impact and not rooted to one specific place.

The Holy Spirit is dynamic. The word translated "power" in the New Testament, and so often linked to the Holy Spirit, is the Greek word dunamis. As well as the word dynamite deriving from this, the word dynamic comes from it too.

So often the Holy Spirit is described in language that implies movement: wind, water, fire, breath. The Spirit of God keeps moving and is far from static. But how does the Spirit makes us more dynamic?

I have had very powerful encounters with the Holy Spirit which have caused me to shake, bounce or feel like electricity pulsing through my body. I have been in many meetings where I have seen the Holy Spirit knock people over, throw them backwards and cause other physical reactions. These are wonderful, exciting, intriguing and thought-provoking experiences. But the dynamic aspect of the power of the Holy Spirit is not limited to such physical manifestations.

If the Holy Spirit transforms us from being static to dynamic, then we would expect to find this characteristic in other areas than just our bodies.

Another area where the Holy Spirit impacts us is in the gifts He gives us. In the New Testament there are three lists of spiritual gifts (or offices) given to the church. They are found in Ephesians 4:11, Romans 12 and 1 Corinthians 12.

The nine gifts in 1 Corinthians 12 are explicitly defined as gifts given by the Spirit. They fall neatly into three groups of three:

- Words of wisdom, words of knowledge and faith
- Healings, works of power and prophecy
- Discernment of spirits, different types of tongues and interpretation of tongues.

All of these are the works of the same Spirit, given to build up the Body of Christ. If we consider that those born of the Spirit become dynamic like the wind, then we might expect that these gifts produce that result.

There are gifts on this list that are obviously "supernatural." These are found in the second two groups of three. We can clearly see how these are dynamic. The same is true of the third group.

However, the first group seems less obviously dynamic - wisdom, knowledge and faith. Given the wider teaching of the New Testament about the Holy Spirit, how do we understand these three gifts? To what extent are they dynamic gifts?

"Words of knowledge" refer to knowledge given supernaturally by the Holy Spirit. This is the gift of knowing things which we have not learned through human means.

The gift of faith is a work of the Spirit. Faith is most clearly defined in Hebrews 11:1.

"Now faith is the assurance of things hoped for, the conviction of things not seen."

Faith has to do with trusting in the unseen. It is the choice to step out of the static world of what is measurable and visible and trust the unseen world of the Spirit.

What about wisdom?

Often our perception of wisdom is that it is static, safe and cautious, grounded, solid and established. We think of wise people as those who take few risks, consider things carefully - those who have learned from the mistakes of youth. If this is what Paul had in mind, then this wisdom that the Holy Spirit gives is solid, safe and dependable, which sounds fairly static to say the least.

But to understand this verse in 1 Corinthians 12, we need to read how Paul understands wisdom in the same letter:

"I was with you in weakness and in fear and much trembling, and my speech and my message were not in plausible words of wisdom, but in demonstrations of the Spirit and of power, that your faith might not rest in the wisdom of men but in the power of God... Yet among the mature we do impart wisdom, although it is not a wisdom of this age or of the rulers of this age, who are doomed to pass away. But we impart a secret and hidden wisdom of God, which God decreed before the ages for our glory." (1 Corinthians 2:3–7)

This definition of wisdom is something wholly different from the cautious, solid wisdom grounded in human learning and experience. Paul directly contrasts the "wisdom of men" with the "power of God." He then claims that the wisdom he imparts as an apostle by the Holy Spirit is "not a wisdom of this age" but a "secret and hidden wisdom of God."

The wisdom which the Spirit gives us is not the wisdom of men. It is the wisdom of God, a secret and hidden wisdom - a wisdom that chose to make itself vulnerable at the cross in order to defeat death; a wisdom that chose weakness to demonstrate great power.

This is the wisdom of an upside-down Kingdom.

Paul goes on to write: "Now we have received not the spirit

of the world, but the Spirit who is from God, that we might understand the things freely given us by God. And we impart this in words not taught by human wisdom but taught by the Spirit, interpreting spiritual truths to those who are spiritual" (1 Corinthians 2:12–13).

The wisdom of God is the impartation of spiritual truths revealed from heaven. It is living by revelation from God even when that seems foolish and ridiculous to our natural thinking. This is a totally different form of wisdom. It is the wisdom that trusts God and His ways, His truth, His perception of reality, rather than the wisdom gained through experiences of life in the natural realm. This is a profoundly dynamic and indeed creative form of wisdom.

My friend Ceri (who had the dream of the green mist) sums this up in a simple way: "Our actions are consistent and rarely change but our characters are inconsistent and constantly changing. God's character never changes but He is infinitely creative and often His actions are different from last time."

The wisdom the Spirit gives provides access to another realm - a wider, greater, unseen, eternal perspective. The children of God are invited to open their ears and eyes to this spiritual wisdom and join in the adventure of a much bigger story that God is writing. They are encouraged not to remain safe and cautious in the static world of human wisdom based on experience.

Hollow religion chooses man-made knowledge and wisdom, putting its trust in what creates a static faith.

Heavenly relationship opts for the spiritual gifts of knowledge and wisdom, putting its trust in what leads to a dynamic momentum – the advance of the Kingdom of Heaven on earth.

## Inheritance Not Wages

The Holy Spirit is God's guarantee that the Gospel is true, that our salvation is real and that an inheritance with our name on it has been set aside in heaven.

The first Christians had met eyewitnesses who had known Jesus and who had experienced extraordinary, miraculous power in their lives. This had brought not only salvation but also a total change of worldview.

In Ephesians 1, Paul describes the Holy Spirit as "the deposit guaranteeing our inheritance until we take possession of it." The important thing to note about this deposit is this: the Holy Spirit impacts the world in ways which we in our own strength could not. He does what we are powerless to do. This is because the gift of the spirit is part of our inheritance given by grace and not something earned by effort.

There are actions, disciplines, habits, which we can embrace that give more space for the Spirit to move in our life but these are only disciplines we apply in order to welcome the Holy Spirit. We remain powerless in our own strength to do the things that only He can do. It is "not by might, nor by power, but by my Spirit, says the LORD of hosts" (Zechariah 4:6).

The Holy Spirit, as a guarantee of our inheritance, gives us His empowering presence for today and a great hope for the future. He also reminds us that God is powerful and we are not, that He is in charge and we are not.

This message resounds throughout the Bible, from the tower of Babel, the birth of Isaac, the dreams and promotion of Joseph, the plagues, the crossing of the Red Sea, the provision of manna, the fall of Jericho, right up to the time of Jesus and beyond. God proves the point to us that He is not asking us to try and do His work for Him but calling us to work in partnership with Him, to see Him do the things on earth that only He can do.

This is our inheritance and the joy of it is that we can rest from striving to earn God's favour, or do His work for Him, both of which are hollow religion.

The Pharisees were vigilant, they knew the Scriptures, they worked hard, they tithed even their herbs and spices and they crossed land and sea to find more converts. But they were driven by hard work and competition and to that extent they were slaves. There isn't a lot of rest in hollow religion.

The Spirit frees us from hollow religion by taking us into rest. In Hebrews 3 and 4 we read about the Sabbath rest for the people of God, drawing on passages in the Old Testament about the Creation and the Exodus. Relationship with God is defined as rest, the place of trust, the place where we no longer have to work to survive or please God.

Rest is only possible where there is trust. If we expect a lilo to sink in a swimming pool, we're unlikely to relax on it. If we are in a crowd at a concert and expect pickpockets to be circulating, then we'll find it hard to relax. If we are sharing a meal with someone who we suspect may lie to us, or verbally attack us, or consciously disagree with everything we say, then it's not a restful experience. The greatest place of rest is the place of trust and security.

A secure child can relax and sleep well when they know their parents are nearby and they are fully protected. I can be myself, can share vulnerably and honestly with those who I trust will love and accept me, even if I share my darkest sins or thoughts. Those who live in dangerous places, war-zones or areas of high crime, can sleep well when they know someone else is alert and responsible for protecting them.

A relationship of trusting God comes from the belief that He is good, that He is loving and that He is powerful. Believing these truths at a heart level releases us into rest.

Knowing that there are things we cannot do and only the Holy Spirit can do, releases us into rest and a more "laid back" life, particularly in the area of ministry.

The Holy Spirit is a deposit guaranteeing our inheritance. This means that the tangible reality of the power of the Holy Spirit releases us to let go of some of the false responsibility we've embraced, trying to do God's job for Him.

Over recent years I have had greater opportunity to watch more closely those who minister effectively in the presence of God and see the Spirit at work in remarkably powerful ways. I have seen close up those who strive and shout and work up a crowd, creating hype, and I have seen those who, with a laid-back approach, have flowed with what the Holy Spirit is doing, unconcerned about criticism, undeterred by a fear of God doing nothing.

The second group are the people who inspire me. There is an ease, a peace, a rest about them. They're not trying to do God's work for Him. They lean into the sovereignty of God and the reality of the Spirit. They trust in the truth that God loves people and likes to heal bodies, mend broken hearts, encourage callings, convict sin, restore hope and sometimes even make His children laugh! We have a guarantee of our inheritance, so we are free to get looser.

## Breathing Fresh Air

The Holy Spirit is the opposite of hollow religion. He is about power not form and revelation not knowledge. He lavishes us with grace when religion whips us with judgment. He is infinitely creative and unrelentingly dynamic, unlike hollow religion, which is stubbornly static, creating a culture of settlers not pioneers. Finally, he is into inheritance not wages, encouraging God's children to rest in what they already have (God's acceptance) rather than strive to earn God's love.

What would you prefer – heavenly relationship with the Holy Spirit or hollow religion?

As we give the Holy Spirit more space to move in our lives, our homes, our workplaces and our churches we will see the green mist of hollow religion displaced by His life-giving oxygen. However, when we choose to cling to form over power, knowledge over revelation, judgment over grace, static tradition over dynamic life, wages over inheritance, we will push Him away and in the process struggle just to survive.

It is time not just to wake up, rise up, cough up, and look up. It's time to fill up.

The Apostle Paul exhorted us to go on being filled with the Holy Spirit (Ephesians 5:18).

Take time to inhale the breath of heaven today.

**Notes:**

i. John Eldredge, *Waking the Dead.*

# 11

# From Discipline to Delight

Throughout the process of turning away from hollow religion into life-giving relationship with God, a number of questions have occurred to me, one of which concerns the relationship between hollow religion and what are known as the spiritual disciplines - such as prayer, fasting, worship, service, solitude, Bible study, and so on.

Are the spiritual disciplines healthy or unhealthy? Put another way, are they just empty religious duties or genuine spiritual exercises? The answer is they can be either, depending on the person performing them. The spiritual disciplines can be either a hollow religious burden or a means for deepening one's relationship with God. It all depends on the heart and motivation of the person concerned.

There are really two dangers here. The first relates to the person who has become free from religion. For such a person there is a danger that tasting grace will cause us to abandon disciplines because of their association with hollow religious duties. When we do that we miss out on the grace-based exercise of the disciplines that leads to deeper intimacy with our loving Father. I know this is true because I've tried life without these disciplines and soon found that my Father is too committed to me flourishing as His son to let me abandon the things that will help me to grow to maturity.

The second danger relates to the person who has not become free from religion. For this person the spiritual disciplines become humanly motivated attempts to bridge the perceived distance between us and God. Instead of engaging in, let us say, prayer as a way of deepening intimacy with the Father, prayer becomes a means of striving to attract God's attention and earn His acceptance. In such a mindset, all the disciplines inevitably gravitate towards drudgery instead of delight.

For some of us spiritual disciplines such as prayer have been taught in a context more akin to law than grace and very often the training has come with external pressure. Our flesh is allergic to discipline and so something greater than fleshly motivation is needed to trump our inclination towards rebellion. When a person is trapped in hollow religion, the only motivation is the "ought" and "should" of religious obligation, usually accompanied by extreme manipulation. When a person is set free into heavenly relationship, this no longer becomes the motivator. The flesh does not drive us. The spirit woos us. So instead of being driven by whips we are led by cords of love. When this happens, activities such as prayer morph from a discipline to a delight.

## Religious Peer Pressure

The trouble with religion is that it can become totally detached from a life-giving relationship with God. The fruit of this is a personal spirituality that is in reality distant from God, one that becomes about "what works for me" rather than intimacy with our Father and our best friend Jesus.

One of the ways we are pulled away from friendship with God is the peer pressure we feel from other Christians who tell us that we should be living our Christian life a certain religious way. Colossians 2:16-19 is a passage that has been very significant for me in this regard. The Colossian church had evidently been infiltrated by a group claiming to be Christians and yet were insisting that they were the real deal because they were more religious in their celebration of Jewish traditions, especially those relating to diet, observing feast days and keeping the Sabbath. Here's what Paul advises:

"Therefore let no one pass judgment on you in questions of food and drink, or with regard to a festival or a new moon or a Sabbath. These are a shadow of the things to come, but the substance belongs to Christ."

This is a passage which has brought me real freedom from religious pressure and into a genuine enjoyment of my relationship with God. Here's a church that has been invaded by a group engaging in external religious pressure tactics. Paul says, "Don't listen to them. It's not about religion. It's about relationship. It's all about Jesus."

Each year I visit the eight to nine year olds at our local school as part of their religious studies. The curriculum requires them to learn about what special food and drink Christians are allowed and what festivals we celebrate, as well as features of church architecture. I tend to cover these as quickly as possible and then let the children ask me any questions they like. Only once in four years has a child asked me about pulpit decorations. All the other questions have been about God. Does He exist? What miracles did Jesus do? Why do I believe it all?

Food and drink, festivals and events, are some of the measurable externals of a religion and when you combine them with the competitive pride of fallen human beings, you have a cocktail of hollow religious pride and criticism.

When certain disciplines develop in one context, if that discipline rather than the source of life becomes the focus, then it's not long before judgment and criticism gets handed out to those who don't do things "properly" i.e. the same way as the enlightened religious elite. The Colossian Christians were being judged by another legalistic group for what they ate and drank and for not observing certain festivals. That is external peer pressure. It is motivated by pride and accompanied by manipulation and control.

As a pastor, I'm regularly asked whether we should do certain religious things. It usually turns out that someone has been pressurised in another context in the same way the Colossian believers were. Here's what Paul goes on to say to those in Colossae who were being made to feel inferior:

"Let no one disqualify you, insisting on asceticism and worship of angels, going on in detail about visions, puffed up without reason by his sensuous mind…"

## Charismatic Boasting

We can see from this that hollow religion isn't limited to boasting about ascetic (i.e. self-denying) acts. At the other end of the spectrum there's boasting about spiritual experiences, such as having visions. Here we see the super-spiritual religious pride which puts others down because they haven't had certain experiences, such as worshipping angels. But angels are created beings, however stunningly majestic they are. Even if an angelic vision or visitation proves life-changing, angels are never to be worshipped. They are servants in God's Kingdom. Worship is for God alone. Boasting of seeing or venerating angels is no cause for self-congratulation!

The same is true for prophetic visions. Visions and dreams are expressions of the God-given gift of prophecy. They are revelations of the mind of Christ given to us by the Holy Spirit. The Bible calls us to steward all the gifts, including prophecy, in a loving way – in a way that strengthens rather than weakens the Church. This means that we do not use our visions as a means of promoting ourselves, nor do we promote such phenomena above and beyond their biblical limits. It is the Giver who is to be exalted, not the gift, and certainly not the one to whom such gifts are given.

See how God's gifts can get abused through an immature excitement that focuses on the hype and drama of experience. A spiritual environment, with a strong culture of grace and a desire to see more supernatural encounters with God, can often experience this immaturity. That isn't a reason to limit grace or shun supernatural experiences. It's a reason for refocusing on the main thing which is not supernatural encounters but our relationship with the Father in heaven.

This is really the lesson Jesus stressed after he sent seventy two disciples out in pairs to preach the Good News of the Kingdom. When they came back buzzing with excitement that they had seen demons submit to them in Jesus' name, Jesus told them not to make that dramatic experience the focus. Jesus realigns them to something far deeper:

"Do not rejoice in this, that the spirits are subject to you, but rejoice that your names are written in heaven" (Luke 10:20).

When we start to emphasize our supernatural successes and neglect to stress relationship with God, the toxic mist of hollow religion has already entered the building.

We must be careful not to wound others with our miracle

success stories, making them feel inferior. And we must be careful when we are hurt by others in this way to take that hurt to Jesus and take heart from the deeper truth that we are God's children and that our names are written in the Father's book.

## Fatherly Wisdom

In Colossians 2 Paul continues, talking about "holding fast to the Head, from whom the whole body, nourished and knit together through its joints and ligaments, grows with a growth that is from God."

Paul now points to the opposite of hollow religion which is "holding fast to the Head," Jesus. The purpose of fasting and feasting, festivals and seasons of discipline, meeting angels and receiving visions, solitude and worshipping with others, is to enable us to hold fast to Jesus, the head of the body (the Church). Like the human body, every part needs direct connection to the brain via the central nervous system. When that connection is lost, then that part of the body becomes numb, lifeless and ceases to function and grow. When the disciplines become disconnected from a vital relationship with Jesus, they become dead duties not living activities.

Rather than abandoning spiritual disciplines we need to remove every trace of hollow religion from them and understand them as our Father's means of training and equipping us to be sons and daughters that know Him deeply and bring His heavenly rule to earth. Seen in this light, the spiritual disciplines are a delight. They are Abba Father's way of equipping us to become mature and productive sons and daughters, helping Him in His family business.

This becomes even clearer when we explore the close link in the Bible between spiritual discipline and God's fatherly wisdom.

The Book of Proverbs is a book full of extraordinary wisdom. It begins with an exhortation to pursue wisdom. From the start the book makes it abundantly clear that acquiring wisdom – a heavenly wisdom designed to empower sons and daughters – is inseparable from discipline.

Proverbs begins with nine chapters of longer discourses, many of which begin with the words, "my son". This can be interpreted at two levels. First of all there's the literal level. The book was written initially as advice to young sons who were setting out into adult life. One way we can best read Proverbs is to see it as parental advice. But then there's a second, spiritual level. If you are not a young man, that doesn't prevent you from reading the book and growing in wisdom. We are God's children, filled with the spirit of sonship, encouraged to call God "Abba, Father" (Galatians 4:4-7; Romans 8:14-17). God addresses us with the words, "my son". Within the context of a trusting relationship of unconditional love with the Father, discipline can lead to a radical increase in wisdom and revelation.

For those who have been set free from hollow religion, the spiritual disciplines are God's fatherly way of drawing us closer into relationship with Him. They are an invitation to turn away from idols and to turn to Him, the source of life. In relationship with Him, we receive revelation from Him.

## Developing Healthy Visions

Everyone has a dream or a vision at some stage in their lives. Young boys dream of scoring a winning goal for England. Pianists dream of playing a Rachmaninov concerto in the Albert Hall. Those dreams either come from within our hearts, as expressions of our own passions, or they derive from external pressure from parents and a desire for their approval.

Spiritual disciplines will become hollow and religious if they are motivated by an insecure desire to earn God's favour. God is not a Father whose approval can be earned from our hard work. We already have His unconditional love and affection. This means that any spiritual discipline, such as prayer or fasting, has to be done from approval not for approval.

The proper basis of engaging in the spiritual disciplines is a vision - a vision of becoming the best son or daughter that we can be. Why do we want to do this? The answer is simple: because God wants to be a Dad to us and He wants us to be His sons and daughters (2 Corinthians 6:18). Everything we do for Him should be designed to deepen this reality.

There is therefore a grace-based way of engaging in the disciplines. We pray, fast, study, serve, worship, give, and all the rest because we are loved not because we want to be loved. We do these things for relational not religious reasons. We do them because we want to become like Jesus, who did these things as expressions of His sonship.

Before starting or continuing with the spiritual disciplines, make sure your vision is properly aligned to God's Word. When the spiritual disciplines are fuelled by a desire to relate more deeply to the Father, to make a valued contribution to the family business, then they will become the means of pursuing deeper intimacy with God and a passion to extend His rule.

That is a good and wholesome vision.

## Cultivating Good Habits

As you begin, let the Holy Spirit woo you into pursuing one or two of the spiritual disciplines. Don't begin because someone has pressurised you to engage in a discipline in order to conform to external peer pressure. Don't begin to compete with the overly-religious or the super-spiritual. Begin because the Father loves you, you love Him, and His grace is calling you to go deeper into His love through these spiritual exercises.

The first time we choose a discipline we are breaking out of an old pattern and forming a habit. The second time is equally hard and then it gradually becomes easier and, after a while, part of the rhythm of our life. If the call is from the Father, then He will give you His grace to empower you to pray more intimately, to fast more sincerely, to give more generously, and so on.

Spiritual disciplines have a cumulative effect. They enable us to build into our lives activities that bring us closer to God, that feed our minds with His truth, that submit our flesh to His purposes. This means that they are not built around our feelings or desires for comfort. They are built on choice and that choice is built on truth.

A religious approach can make the form the priority - the number of days fasted, the number of hours prayed, the number of donations given, the number of Bible passages read. Don't be controlled by form or structure, by appearance or reputation. When this happens all your effort goes into getting it right. Driven by the fear of breaking the habit, you become a slave to superstition.

As we saw in Colossians 2, our focus can shift from worshipping God to being controlled by a calendar and keeping festivals. We are not to be driven by "ought" and "must." We are to be led by the Father's love into a greater, deeper, longer pursuit of His heart using these spiritual exercises.

## Receiving Great Rewards

Two of the greatest sportsmen of my generation have been David Beckham (football) and Johnny Wilkinson (rugby). They could kick more consistently and accurately than anyone else in the

UK and by doing so brought joy to millions in key moments in sporting contests.

Were they both hugely naturally talented? Yes.

Did they both work hard for hours and hours practising? Yes. Respective coaches have commented on their extraordinary work ethic and discipline. A few years ago a sports company made an advert showing them both out practising kicking and kicking and kicking through driving rain, wind, snow and baking sunshine, early in the morning and on after dusk. If you're not into sport, then pick an example from concert pianists or world class chefs (without the wind and rain!).

To become exceptional requires consistent discipline combined with natural gifts. Johnny Wilkinson and David Beckham would have been average professional sportsmen if they hadn't engaged in unseen discipline on the training ground.

This comes down to a basic choice for all of us. Do I choose to stay in bed or on the sofa watching TV? Or do I choose to get up and go out in the rain and practice kicking a ball between sticks? The response to that choice will be motivated in all sorts of ways, including our visions and our habits. To be disciplined means to say no to the thing that is comfortable or easy, in order to say yes to the challenge that will make us more fully alive. I don't know for sure but I imagine that David Beckham and Johnny Wilkinson at some level actually enjoy the action of kicking a ball just as most concert pianists enjoy sitting at piano making music. There are times of repetition for fitness or playing scales but the basic driver for the discipline is pleasure and enjoyment.

This is essential when we consider spiritual disciplines. The religious attitude is that we are "doing things which we don't enjoy because they're good for us" (like eating vegetables as a child). But as God's children spiritual disciplines are choosing to say no to what's easy and comfortable in order to do the things that connect us with God.

Praying, reading the Bible, fasting, solitude, worship all require us to say no to thinking about ourselves. They require us to say no to the passive consumption of entertainment. As we say no to these things, we find ways to reconnect with God that bring great pleasure to the soul. They enable us to transition from discipline to delight.

There is no doubt that David Beckham and Jonny Wilkinson have received great public adulation and extraordinary financial benefit. All their hard work has been done from a place of fun and has led to more fun. But never forget that their public reward was a result of their private dedication. The visible benefits came from invisible sacrifices.

So it is with us. Jesus says in Matthew 6 that the Father alone sees what and when we pray in the secret place, in the unseen private world of intimacy with Him. As we develop a vision for doing this out of love, and as we cultivate good habits inspired by the Holy Spirit, we enjoy His presence more and more, unseen by anyone except Him.

But all this is not in vain. There are rewards for those who engage in such unseen disciplines. These may not be public adoration or great wealth, as they have been for sports personalities or famous musicians. But they will be the indescribable, invisible and unending riches of the amazing grace and lavish love of God. Money cannot buy that.

Fame and fortune cannot compete with it either.

So, in answer to our question at the start of this chapter, spiritual disciplines in and of themselves are not good or evil. They are neutral.

Religious people will use them to make themselves look better before God and others. So will super-spiritual people who stress the supernatural experiences these exercises have provided.

When this happens, the spiritual disciplines have become a negative reality.

But the grace-based person who is free from hollow religion has a totally different motivation. He or she is not motivated by external control or a desire to earn God's favour but by a desire to connect more deeply with the God of love and to enjoy Him not only in the here-and-now but forever and ever.

When this is the motivation, discipline before long turns to delight.

# 12

# The Power of Love

The solution to hollow religion is reconciliation with the Father in a relationship of love. I have attempted to show that so much of what God reveals about His Kingdom in the Bible is the opposite of hollow religion. The greatest antidote to hollow religion is love. It is love that sets us free. It is love that restores and releases us. Love is the primary characteristic of the Kingdom of God; without it hollow religion thrives.

In 1 Corinthians 13:1-3 the Apostle Paul declares:

"If I speak in the tongues of men and of angels, but have not love, I am a noisy gong or a clanging cymbal. And if I have prophetic powers, and understand all mysteries and all knowledge, and if I have all faith, so as to remove mountains, but have not love, I am nothing. If I give away all I have, and if I deliver up my body to be burned, but have not love, I gain nothing."

The enemy's scheme of hollow religion is based on lies that deny the love of God and when we believe those lies, it causes us to live lives which do not express God's love. Love is powerful, gracious, dynamic, relational and establishes covenant family relationships.

The purpose of getting hollow religion out of our lives isn't to make our lives more exciting (although it will!) or more comfortable (it won't!), nor is it to make us safer, healthier or richer. It is to enable us as children of God to demonstrate the Father's love to a hurting, lost world. It is to build churches which worship God in a way that goes beyond personal preference. In such churches worship becomes a desire to honour and exalt Him and encounter Him, to enable God's children to partner with Him in prayer to establish His Kingdom rule on earth as it is in the heavenly realms. Such churches are characterised not by division and criticism, or by judgement or politics, but by joy, fun and overflowing love.

You are a beloved child of God. Turn from judgement to grace. Let go of being static and cautious. Become "looser." Take your eyes off the outward form of things around you and look for signs of God's power. Choose to live by revelation and not rely just on your own knowledge. And as a beloved child of God give up trying to earn wages from Him and simply enjoy your inheritance.

God has called us to partner with Him in building the family business. When He established the mandate for this, He did so in a way that made relationship with Him the foundation. In Matthew 28:18-20 He promised to be with us as we do so:

"All authority in heaven and on earth has been given to me. Go therefore and make disciples of all nations, baptising them in the name of the Father and of the Son and of the Holy Spirit, teaching them to observe all that I have commanded you. And behold, I am with you always, to the end of the age."

From now on, choose relationship over religion.

# Appendix: How to Recognise Hollow Religion

I have found these simple checklists a helpful tool to recognise hollow religion in my life, in order to throw it off, turn to God for forgiveness and then replace it with Kingdom choices. No one else needs to see these lists – they are for you and God to reflect on together. There is a checklist for each of the contrasts we have explored in this book:

• Form without power
• Knowledge not revelation
• Judgement not grace
• Static not dynamic
• Wages not inheritance.

## Form Without Power

☐ I think style matters and will turn people to God.

☐ I spend more time than I'd like thinking about my reputation.

☐ I would never go to church looking a mess.

☐ I believe that if a church doesn't look cool, then it'll never grow.

☐ Sometimes when worshipping, others may think I look spiritual but I'm actually preoccupied with something else other than God.

☐ I quite like people to see my acts of service.

☐ In some ways I'd quite like church to be a club of people I find easy to relate to.

☐ Too often I catch myself judging people.

☐ Motives don't matter; we've got a job to do and so if I can get people to serve that's what matters.

☐ I make a huge effort to be right so no one can reject me as stupid.

☐ There are areas of my life that I am totally ashamed of. I could never confess them even to those I trust because they'd think less of me.

## Knowledge Not Revelation

How do we recognise when knowledge has displaced revelation? The root lie undergirding the quest for knowledge is the belief that knowledge will give us power and autonomy. When the desire for knowledge arises, ask yourself questions such as,

• Why do I need to know this?
• What will I gain from knowledge about this?
• Is there anyone I'm subconsciously trying to compete with through knowledge in this area?

Other characteristics of knowledge to look out for:

☐ I feel uncomfortable if I don't know about a subject.

☐ There are certain subjects or topics I feel I have "ownership" of because I know about them.

☐ "I know all about…"

☐ My academic studies have given me a good foundation for ministry.

☐ I feel inadequate alongside those who have studied more than me.

☐ I don't have confidence to preach on a subject unless I know a certain amount about it.

Are you led by analysis or revelation? Ask yourself these questions:

☐ What were the last 5 decisions I made?

☐ What process did I follow to make them?

☐ In what ways did I seek God for revelation?

Some other questions to consider in recognising analysis taking precedence over listening to God:

☐ Do I accept counsel from those who I recognise have prophetic gifts or do I only trust intelligent, analytical people?

☐ Do I believe that I can hear God's voice on major decisions?

☐ Am I seeking to grow in my ability to hear God speak in a variety of ways?

☐ Do I wake up in the night turning things around in my head, or worrying about the potential implications of risky steps of faith I've taken?

☐ Am I afraid that God won't speak to me?

## Judgement Not Grace

How do we recognise when judgement has displaced grace?

☐ Next time you preach/teach/minister publicly, be alert to how much energy you put into defending yourself from criticism.

☐ Choose not to make any judgements about anyone for a whole day.

☐ When you find yourself in a conversation which is spiralling into judgement or criticism, see what positive, honouring comments you can make to reverse that spiral.

Tick any of the following boxes if you recognise any of these statements appearing regularly in your life:

## Judgement

☐ That's not the right way to do it.

☐ My way is better.

☐ I've been through "that one."

☐ Do as I say, not as I do.

☐ My church is the best/at the cutting edge.

☐ Why would anyone do that?

☐ I'm glad I'm not part of that church; it doesn't do what we're doing.

☐ None of this is applicable to me/us.

☐ I never miss a Sunday service.

☐ Who are you to challenge me?

☐ You need to hear the teaching on…

☐ If only others were like us.

☐ They really shouldn't do that.

☐ They're heading in the wrong direction with that decision.

## Fear of Criticism

☐ I particularly care what (name the person) thinks of me because they're powerful, spiritual, rich etc.

☐ I'm particularly careful how I present myself to (N).

☐ I join in, rather than initiate.

☐ I only say what people want to hear.

☐ I play my cards close to my chest.

☐ I allow myself to be defined by who people say I am.

☐ I fear lack of recognition from those in authority over me.

☐ I don't have much to offer.

## Static or Dynamic?

How do we recognise ourselves becoming static?

☐ I am proud of my knowledge of certain traditions and history.

☐ I spend a considerable amount of my energy on preserving or recovering aspects of the past.

☐ I fear change.

☐ My initial reaction to news of unfamiliar Christian movements is suspicion and I search for errors or things to criticise.

☐ My life (internal and external) looks a lot now like it did five years ago.

☐ I avoid change in my church, because it would bring a bad reaction.

☐ I believe the church exists to hold ground and stem the tide of secularisation.

## Wages Not Inheritance

☐ I often make assumptions about what will please God, without asking Him.

☐ I fear that if I don't tithe/serve/pray/read my Bible, God won't protect my finances/health/family and disasters will happen.

☐ There's a lot of "ought" and "must" in my life.

☐ When I sin, I don't feel I can approach God and be intimate with him until I've pursued certain disciplines, (prayer of confession, reading the Bible, tithing, worship, going to church...)

☐ When I get raw, honest and angry with God, I remind him of all my sacrifices/efforts/good works as grounds for Him to bless me.

☐ I don't really believe the resources of heaven are available to me.

☐ I see myself more as God's servant than as his son/daughter.

☐ It takes me a long time to feel close to God again after I've done something I feel guilty about.

# Further Reading

Repenting of Religion – Greg Boyd (Baker Publishing Group)

Benefit of the Doubt – Greg Boyd (Baker Publishing Group)

Center Church – Timothy Keller (Zondervan)

The Prodigal God – Timothy Keller (Hodder & Stoughton)

I Am Your Father – Mark Stibbe (Monarch)

The End of Religion – Bruxy Cavey (NavPress Publishing Group)

Ethics – Diethrich Bonhoeffer (Augsburg Fortress)

What's So Amazing About Grace? – Philip Yancey (Zondervan)

Velvet Elvis – Rob Bell (Collins)

Blue Like Jazz – Donald Miller (Thomas Nelson)

Sacrifice and the Death of Christ – Frances Young (Wipf and Stock)

The Conservative Soul – Andrew Sullivan (Harper Perennial)

Waking the Dead – John Eldredge (Thomas Nelson)

Discipleship – David Watson (Hodder Paperbacks)

The Shack – William P Young (Hodder & Stoughton)

The Shack Revisited – C. Baxter Kruger (Hodder Paperbacks)

Freedom From the Religious Spirit – C.Peter Wagner (Regal Books)

Overcoming the Religious Spirit – Rick Joyner (Morningstar Publications)